Festival of Remembrance and Hope

Festival of Remembrance and Hope

John Williams

FESTIVAL OF REMEMBRANCE AND HOPE
By: John Williams
Copyright © 2010
GOSPEL FOLIO PRESS
All Rights Reserved

Published by
GOSPEL FOLIO PRESS
304 Killaly St. W.
Port Colborne, ON L3K 6A6
CANADA

ISBN: 9781926765259

Cover design by Danielle Elzinga

All Scripture quotations from the
King James Version unless otherwise noted.

Printed in USA

Dedication

To the many Christians through whose prayers,
guidance and fellowship my life has been enriched.

Author's Preface

Today there appears to be a tension in evangelical circles, between the emphasis placed on Bible teaching and evangelism on the one hand, and an appreciation of the Lord's Supper on the other. In Catholic and other sacramental circles, the celebration of the Eucharist tends to win out over the proclamation of the Word. Attendance at Mass is paramount, sometimes even above personal faith and practical Christian living.

It was this sort of thing that roused the Reformers to challenge Christendom and to announce the importance and authority of Scripture as well as congregational worship at the Lord's Supper. The Reformers were right of course, but what of us their spiritual heirs? Are we in danger of adopting a position where we stand for the supremacy of the Word but fail to give the Lord's s Supper the prominence it deserves? For all their divergent eucharistic interpretations, Wycliffe, Luther, Calvin and Zwingli had this in common, they were men of the Book as well as, men of the Table. They were expositors and they were worshippers.

In our experience-oriented society we certainly need to be confronted and nourished by the objective truth of Scripture, the only safe beacon of spiritual life and hope. But, we also need to match our enthusiasm for the Word with a commitment to obey Christ's ordinances. After all, the One who said, *"Search the Scriptures, they testify of Me;"* also said, *"Do this in remembrance of Me"* (John 5:39; Luke 22:19). Obedience ceases to be obedience when it becomes selective. In any case, our submission to the Word is born of our submission to Christ.

Hopefully, this little book will help redress the balance for some. The Word and the Table go together. They are both proclamations of God's good news for us sinners, the one oral, the other visual and dynamic. Divorced from each other, each loses something of its wonder: together they bring us to our knees, first in repentance and faith, then in worship and thanksgiving for so great a Saviour and "so great salvation".

The reader of these pages will quickly discover that there is no championing of sacerdotalism or sacramentalism here; nor any support for lazy conformity. Our desire is to be irenic and charitable, while not watering down the plain teaching of the Scriptures of truth. We believe it is time to stir our resolve and to have done with all the stultifying effects of ecclesiastical traditions, no matter how we may admire their exponents.

Let us encourage all the members of the Body of Christ to exercise their gifts, rather than sit in a 'comfortable pew' with the attitude, " We'll pay the shot, while you do the job up front, on our behalf." With the Word of God in our hands, and the love of Christ in our hearts, let us come to the Lord's Supper with a renewed determination to give expression to our worship and to give the Lord the praise that belongs to Him alone. There is surely a wealth of understanding in the simple line of the old spiritual: "Let us break bread together on our knees!"

Victoria, B.C., 2010

Contents

Part 1

Getting Things In Perspective

"The bread and wine are spread upon the board,
The guests are here, invited by the Lord;
Why come they thus, why tarry for a space?
 But for Thy presence, O Thou King of grace.

Hush , O our hearts, as in the sacred Name
We bow in worship and Thy presence claim-
Where two or three are gathered there am I,
Unseen, yet present to faith's opened eye.

Here in our midst art Thou, O Risen Lord;
Worthy, O Lamb once slain; to be adored;
Here in our midst to lead Thy people's praise,
And incense sweet unto the Father raise.

We do remember Thee, as Thou hast said,
And think upon Thee as we break the bread,
Recall Thy dying love, Thy Cross and shame,
Drinking the cup of blessing in Thy name."

George Goodman (1866 – 1944)

Chapter 1

Names for the Lord's Supper

There are two Christian ordinances according to the New Testament, namely, Baptism and the Lord's Supper. Both are symbolical and both give dramatic, visual witness to the death, burial and resurrection of the Lord Jesus Christ. While baptism is initiatory, witnessing to our salvation and incorporation into the Body of Christ; the Lord's Supper nourishes our on-going fellowship in that Body. These ordinances are therefore, expressions both of our personal faith and corporate relationships in Christ.

In the following chapters we shall be particularly concerned with the ordinance of the Lord's Supper, considering its institution, its significance and meaning, as well as its contemporary relevance and celebration. We will also take a brief look at the development of eucharistic doctrine in the course of church history, particularly since the Reformation, in order to learn from the discoveries, courage, struggles and mistakes of earlier generations. While we do not accept the various ecclesiastical traditions as normative or authoritative in the same way we regard Scripture, they do offer theological perspective and some understanding of different church practices. In fact, it is clear that many of the extra-biblical terms frequently used to describe the Lord's Supper, grow directly out of these various traditions.

New Testament Terms

The Lord's Supper

This term, most widely used among Protestant congregations,

occurs only once in the New Testament, in 1 Corinthians 11:23. There, it translates Paul's words, *kuriakos deipnon* (literally, 'the Lordly Supper') deipnon was the regular term for the main meal served at the end of the work day.

The lateness of the hour of the Last Supper is suggested by two other things. First, there are the words of the apostle, *"The Lord Jesus, the same night in which he was betrayed"*. Second, there is the association of the Lord's Supper with the Passover which was a family meal usually enjoyed in the evening (cf. Matt. 26:26ff, Mark 14:22ff, Luke 22:14ff, cf. Acts. 20:2ff).

The Communion

The word 'communion' is one of several translations of the Greek word *koinōnia* (others include, *"fellowship"* -Acts 2:42; *"contribution"* Rom. 15:26, *"participation"* 1 Cor. 10:16 NIV). This Greek word stresses the idea of, 'having a share in' and is derived from *koinos*, meaning, 'common' (cf. Titus. 1 :4). The title, "The Communion" derives from Paul's question in 1 Corinthians 10:16, (KJV), *"Is it not the communion of the blood... the body of Christ?"* The apostle does not insert the definite article before the noun, *koinōnia*, nor does he give the word the official sense it has acquired in ecclesiastical circles. However familiar we are with the terms, "the Communion" or "the Holy Communion," they are not strictly speaking, biblical terms but represent accepted Christian tradition.

The Breaking of Bread

The term, 'breaking of bread' is peculiar to Luke's writings in the New Testament. He mentions it first in his description of the meal Jesus shared with the two disciples at Emmaus, on the evening of Resurrection Day (cf. Luke 24:35). However "sacred" that meal became in the memory of those two disciples, it seems that their original intent was simply to invite a stranger in for an ordinary evening meal. They certainly had not planned a communion service, although their hospitality brought unexpected and remarkable dividends.

Luke also uses the verb, 'to break bread,' when describing the sacred meal the early Christians celebrated, as an expression of their communal fellowship on the first day of the week (Acts 2:42). It is interesting to note that in Luke 24:35 and Acts 2:42, the definite article is used (*tē klasei tou artou*). The verb, 'to break bread' which incidentally; is used of Jesus' feeding of the multitude, was regularly used among Jews to describe sharing in a common meal (cf. Matt. 4:19,14:36). Even today, in many Jewish homes, the weekly, Friday evening meal begins with the *Kiddush* or 'blessing,' followed by a, 'breaking of bread.' Usually, on this occasion, the host takes a matzos cracker, breaks it, then shares it with all who are seated around the table.

It was natural that the early Christians, who of course were Jews, would use the phrase, 'breaking of bread' to characterize both their secular and religious meals. Something else to keep in mind is that the breaking of bread and the *agapē* ('love feast') were apparently linked together in early church practice (cf. Jude v.12). Even today, in less structured, evangelical Christian churches, people prefer to use the term, 'breaking of bread' when describing their weekly communion.

The Eucharist

Although not used by New Testament writers, the word Eucharist does have its roots in their language. It is really a transliteration of the Greek word *eucharistia* which means 'thanksgiving.' The cognate verb *eucharisteō* is used in several passages where the Lord's Supper is in view. For example, in Matthew's institution narrative we read, "Then he took the cup, gave thanks (*eucharistēsas*) and offered it to them, saying, *"drink from it all of you"* (Matt. 26:27; Luke22:17-19). Paul writes similarly, *"The Lord Jesus, on the night He was betrayed, took bread and when He had given thanks (euchristēsas), He broke it... "* (1 Cor. 11:24).

It is unfortunate that the term, The Eucharist tends to have such strong sacerdotal overtones today, especially since, in the institution narratives, it has the sense of a simple "thank you". What could be more fitting in any remembrance service than giving thanks? Perhaps we should call the Lord's Supper, 'The

Thanksgiving.' This would escape the undue sacramentalism of the word Eucharist yet recapture the essential simplicity of the Supper as celebrated by the earliest Christians.

Alan Stibbs, an Anglican minister, explains, "If we use the term eucharist or eucharistic sacrifice to describe the sacrament as a whole, we conceal thereby its primary character as the Lord's Supper or Gospel feast. We ought therefore not to speak of going to the eucharist, nor of offering the eucharistic sacrifice but of sharing in the administration of the Lord's Supper..." [1]

The Lord's Table

While this expression, found in I Corinthians 10:21, is often used to describe a communion service, it appears to have a wider connotation for the apostle Paul. For him, just as, "the table of demons" stood for involvement in an idolatrous, pagan life-style, so the title, "Table of the Lord" signified, fellowship in the local church and a Christian life-style. Having said that however, it would certainly not be inappropriate to describe participation in the Lord's Supper as, "being present at the Lord's Table." It would perhaps encourage a more inclusive spirit than that displayed by some Christians who appear to see it as "our table."

Other Related Terms

Ordinance

We are using the word 'ordinance' here, not in the broader dictionary definition of, 'religious rite' but in the more focused sense of, something *"ordained by Christ."* The New Testament makes it quite clear that both believer's baptism and the Lord's Supper were instituted and ordained by Christ, to be observed by his followers in all future generations (Matt. 29:19-20).

---

1   A.M.Stibbs, *Sacrament, Sacrifice and Eucharist*. Tyndale Press, London 1961.
p.39

Sacrament

It is too bad that the word 'sacrament' has taken on such mystical, sacerdotal overtones in many circles. The word itself comes from the Latin *sacramentum*, which described among other things, the oath of allegiance sworn by a Roman soldier when he enlisted in the army and pledged to be faithful to his captain. If we wish to describe the Lord's Supper as a 'sacrament,' in that sense, that is to say, to affirm our being Christ's faithful and obedient promise-keepers, so well and good! However, that is not the way the word is generally used in more traditional ecclesiastical settings. In circles where the word Sacrament is regularly used it tends to imply that the bread and wine are "spiritual signs" of the real presence of Christ's Body and Blood.

The Remembrance Meeting

In many less structured churches where the Lord's Supper is celebrated weekly, it is often described as, the 'Remembrance Meeting'. This term along with another, 'the Worship Meeting', is generally used among a group of churches known as, Christian Brethren. Now, while remembrance and worship should be prominent features in any celebration of the Lord's Supper, they should surely characterize the rest of our lives as well. The Saviour Himself makes it abundantly clear in His conversation with the woman of Samaria, that worship is a matter of heart attitude, not something to be limited to any particular time or place (cf. John 4). Of course, there should be a special emphasis on remembrance at the Lord's Supper since that is the special point the Lord makes in His words of institution.

"The Sacrifice Of The Mass"

This description of the Lord's Supper which reflects neither New Testament practice nor intent, is used mainly, though not exclusively, in the Roman Catholic Church and is germane to its peculiar eucharistic theology In fact, it is not only a distinctive element of Catholic eucharistic teaching but the "great divide" between Catholicism and Protestantism. We include reference to it here for two reasons. First, to serve as a warning about the dangers of substituting humanly contrived religious theories for the plain truth of Scripture. Second, it is a reminder that if we fail to learn from the mistakes of history, how ever cleverly they are disguised, we may end up making them all over again.

Although, a distinction is drawn between the "Sacrifice of the Mass" and the "Mass," in common parlance, the two are practically synonymous. Roman Catholic teaching declares quite unequivocally that in the Mass the priest offers an "unbloody sacrifice" of Christ which is efficacious for the forgiveness of the sins of the living and the dead as well. This of course, is all part and parcel of the doctrine of transubstantiation, which was officially promulgated by the Council of Trent in the sixteenth century.

These then are some of the more common terms used to describe the Lord's Supper. Each, with the exception of the name, "the Mass," represents some aspect of biblical teaching. While it is vital to distinguish between biblical and traditional descriptions of the Lord's Supper, the important thing is not what we call it but appreciating why we celebrate it and to be spiritually prepared. As we conclude this opening chapter we recall the famous words of Martin Luther:

> "We accept this Sacrament or Testament or Blessing
> - as in Latin, or Eucharist as in Greek, or the
> Table of the Lord, or Lord's Supper, or the Lord's
> Memorial, or Communion, or by whatever name
> you please, as long as it is not polluted by the name
> of sacrifice or work."

Chapter 2

Suggested Antecedents

The Lord's Supper, as its name suggests, was instituted by Christ Himself on the eve of His Passion. He evidently intended it as a *"living memorial"* of Himself and of His all-sufficient, redeeming sacrifice. Every time Christians participate in this special meal, they have before them visible, tangible memorials of their Lord. However, there is more here since both the bread and the cup have their own historical and spiritual significance.

Most Bible scholars agree that while the Lord's Supper is unique, it is not entirely without meaningful antecedents, especially in Jewish thought and tradition. It will be helpful therefore, to look briefly at some of these. As we do so we should remind ourselves that table fellowship among the Jews and other Middle Eastern peoples has sacred as well as social aspects. Hence, the importance of giving thanks or, as we describe it, "saying grace". To break table fellowship has always been considered a reprehensible thing For example, the Psalmist writes, *"Even my close friend, whom I trusted, he who shared my bread, has lifted up his heel against me"* (Ps. 41:9). These words were actually quoted by Jesus regarding Judas' defection, on the occasion of the meal as described in John's Gospel (cf. John 13:18).

The Dead Sea Scrolls indicate that the ancient Essene community at Qumran began and ended its daily communal meals with bread and wine, over which a special blessing had been spoken. Even today, in orthodox Jewish circles, the sharing of bread and wine has particular cultural, if not religious significance (see Gen. 14:18). The following practices are sometimes viewed as historical and religious antecedents of the Christian feast of remembrance.

The Memorial Supper for the Departed

The Jewish custom of giving a cup of wine (the cup of consolation) to a mourner, and the sharing of a meal in honour of a deceased friend or relative are seen by some as part of the cultural background of the Lord's Supper. The words of the prophet Jeremiah, *"Neither will men break bread in mourning for them, to comfort anyone for the dead, nor give them a cup of consolation to drink for anyone's father or mother"*- are cited in support of this view (cf. Jer. 16:7; see also Ezek. 24:17,22).

However, although at first sight the prophet's words might appear to have a bearing on Jesus' supper, on closer consideration, this connection is tenuous indeed. After all, Christ was still alive when He instituted His memorial feast! As Christians we do not commemorate a dead Christ: we worship a living Saviour! There could hardly be a greater contrast, than that between a wake (whether Jewish or Irish) and a Christian celebration of the Lord's Supper.

While it may be true that the elements of bread and wine speak of the sacrificial giving of the body and blood of Christ on the cross, the Lord's Supper is essentially, a "live remembrance" of the risen Christ. We should not mournfully brood on His death but joyfully exult in His resurrection and coming. Christians do not break bread as mourners at a funeral, but as grateful worshippers celebrating their Saviour's triumph. We certainly show no lack of appreciation of Christ's sufferings — quite the contrary. However, we recognize that true worship sees the cross in the light of the empty tomb. We can never over-emphasize the Saviour's words, *"Remember Me"*. He certainly did not say, "lament My death!" We should keep in mind Paul's significant word to the Corinthians, *"let us keep festival"* (*heortazōmen*) (1 Cor. 5:8). Incidentally, this same Greek verb is used in the Septuagint version of the Old Testament in connection with the Passover, which was certainly a celebratory occasion.

Sacrificial Meals

Some see the ritual meal associated with the various ancient, Jewish sacrificial ceremonies as a precursor of the Lord's Supper, particularly with its emphasis on communion. However, while the Levitical system allowed the offerer to participate in the sacrificial meal, as for example in the so-called "sweet offerings," there is no suggestion of this being a meal shared with God (see Lev. 7: 15-21; Deut. 12:5-7). The worshipper while said to be "eating before the Lord", is never said to be "eating with the Lord." In fact, a careful reading of the sacrificial regulations reveals that God's portion of the sacrifice was usually burned on the altar. Certain parts of some offerings were given to the priests but not to be consumed at "ritual meals". These gifts were simply payment in kind for services rendered (see Lev. 7:8-10; 24:5-9; Matt. 12:4).

Certainly, the writer of the Epistle to the Hebrews tells us that there are many beautiful types in the Levitical rituals and offerings. However, it takes a large stretch of the imagination to see any parallels between those Old Testament sacrificial procedures and the simple atmosphere and intent of the Lord's Supper. When Jesus used the expression, *"the new covenant (hē kainē diathēkē) in My blood"*, at the Last Supper, He was not so much comparing as contrasting the old rituals and the new blessings He secured by His saving death.

The Sinai Covenant Meal

This Old Testament story has also been cited as having a bearing on the Lord's Supper (cf. Ex. 24:9-11). There, we read how Moses, Aaron, Nadab, Abihu and the seventy elders of Israel enjoyed a unique religious experience *"they saw God and they ate and drank"*. Now although no eucharistic lessons are drawn from this "cultic meal," by the New Testament writers, Moses' statement, *"This is the blood of the covenant that the Lord has made with you in accordance with all these words"* certainly sounds significant in light of Our Lord's words of institution.(Ex. 24:8).

While there may be an association of ideas here, we should

FESTIVAL OF REMEMBRANCE & HOPE

be careful not to read too much into this story. We have a similar linking of ideas in connection with a fellowship meal described as the *"cutting of a covenant,"* in Genesis 18:7-10 (see also: Gen. 31:44-46; Ex. 12:7-8,18: 7-121; I Sam. 11:14-15).

As the disciples sat at the table sharing a meal with their Master, who was no less a Person than *"God manifest in flesh,"* they heard Him say among other things, *"This cup is the new covenant in My blood, which is poured out for you"* (Luke 22:20). It is possible that some among them would remember the story from Exodus 24. The significance of Jesus' words would not be lost on them.

The Feasts of Jehovah

Israel's various festivals were not only occasions for the corporate worship of Jehovah, but opportunities for congregational celebration and ceremonial feasting. Indeed, in some cases specific dietary and culinary arrangements are included in the festival regulations (see Ex. 23: 14-19; Lev. 23: 1-44; Num. 28:1-29 & 40). A couple of other factors may have some bearing on our subject. First, these Old Testament festivals have their roots in history and tend to be commemorative in character. Second, certain ethical requirements are implied. For example, only those members of the congregation who are ceremonially and morally clean are invited to participate. Paul certainly has this sort of thing in mind when, in the context of his eucharistic teaching he writes: *"Do not be idolaters, as some of them were; as it is written: The people sat down to eat and drink and got up to indulge in pagan revelry."* (1 Cor.10:7; cf. Ex. 32:6). He is certainly making the point that worship cannot be divorced from morality.

The Passover Meal

While we need not accept the Pascal theory which sees the Lord's Supper simply as a Christianized Passover, obviously these two feasts share common features. For example, both are commemorative; both are congregationally celebrated; both are forward looking; and both have clear ethical requirements (see

22

1 Cor. 5: 6-8). But clearly, there are striking differences and these should not be overlooked.

The Synoptic institution narratives in particular show these differences between our Lord's celebration of the Passover and His Supper. It appears from those Gospels that Jesus deliberately ate His Passover one day early. This is reflected in His words: *"I have earnestly and intensely desired to eat this Passover with you before I suffer; for I say to you, I shall eat it no more until it is fulfilled in the kingdom of God."* (Luke 22:15-16 AMP).

His reason for this arrangement was the fact that He Himself was to be offered as God's Pascal lamb on Passover Day. This idea is supported by both the Johannine and Pauline narratives (see John 19: 36 and I Cor. 5:6-8). It is obvious that although the Lord's Supper was instituted at a Passover meal and in a sense, grew out of it, the two meals are quite distinct. We will discuss their relationship in more detail in following chapters.

Melchizedek's Gift to Abraham

Another event sometimes regarded as an symbolic type anticipating the Lord's Supper, is the Old Testament story of Melchisedek's gift of bread and wine brought to Abraham on the occasion of his victory over King Chedorlaomer and his allies (see, Genesis 14). However, although the elements of bread and wine given by this King-Priest were the same as those used by the Lord Jesus in His Supper, any connection between these occasions is not altogether obvious. At least we might see the bread and wine of this Genesis story as celebratory gifts brought to commemorate a great victory. In this sense we might see a link. After all, whenever we participate in the Lord's Supper we remember our Saviour and celebrate His great victory over death, "the last enemy!" It is perhaps worth noting that although Melchizedek's story is referred to in the New Testament, nothing is mentioned of his gift, only of Abraham's tithes and our Lord's eternal priesthood *"according to the order of Melchizedek"* (see Heb. 7:1ff.). Perhaps therefore we should be careful in seeing a type of the Lord's Supper here where Scripture itself does not.

Malachi's "pure offering"

Before leaving this subject of possible antecedents which may or may not have a bearing on the Lord's Supper, one other passage calls for attention. It is Malachi's prophecy, *"For from the rising of the sun even unto the going down of the same My Name is great among the Gentiles; and in every place incense is offered unto My Name, and a pure offering: for My Name is great among the Gentiles said the Lord of hosts."* (Mal. 1:11 RV).

Although the connection is not immediately obvious, ever since the time of the Didachē (c. A.D. 100), this Old Testament passage has been cited as having eucharistic significance, particularly in those circles where the Lord's Supper is described as "a sacrifice". However, what is in view, in both Malachi and the Didachē, are "spiritual sacrifices". Malachi's words surely have very little to do with the Lord's Supper. Even if we accept that the Prophet is predicting something in the distant future, the New Testament nowhere cites his words as having any relevance as far as the Lord's Supper is concerned. In fact, the RV text - following the Septuagint - uses the present tense "is," rather than the future , "shall be," in Malachi 1:11. This suggests that Malachi, like Isaiah, Amos and other inspired spokesmen, is challenging his contemporaries' to abandon their empty ceremonialism, for true worship. His point is, that despite Israel's fastidious ceremonialism, God has rejected their sacrifices. The Lord desires a right heart attitude, rather than mere repetition of empty, sacrificial ceremonies. In startling contrast, Malachi says that despite Israel's failure and the emptiness of her religion, God's name *"is great among the Gentiles; and in every place incense is offered unto His name and a pure offering"*. So much then for these "suggested antecedents."

Chapter 3

The Lord's Supper
and the Passover

New Testament Evidence

Before examining the Passover Seder "our feast of Redemption", as the Jews call it and noting the parallels between it and the Lord's Supper, we will look briefly at some New Testament scriptures to help chart our course. For example, the Synoptists all see the Last Supper against its Paschal backdrop. Matthew writes, *"On the first day of the Feast of Unleavened Bread, the disciples came to Jesus and asked, 'Where do You want us to make preparations for You to eat the Passover?' He replied, 'Go into the city to a certain man and tell him, "The Teacher says: My appointed time is near. I am going to celebrate the Passover with My disciples at your house."' So the disciples did as Jesus had directed them and prepared the Passover."* (Matt. 26:17-19; see also Mark 14:12-26; Luke 22:7-23). Matthew goes on to tell us that Jesus instituted His own supper, during the Passover meal (vv. 20-30).

Although John does not specifically identify the meal as the Seder and suggests a slightly different time-table, he is clearly thinking about Jesus as the Paschal Lamb. He writes: *"It was just before the Passover Feast. Jesus knew that the time had come for Him to leave this world and go to the Father.... The evening meal was being served... so He got up from the meal... and began to wash His disciples' feet, drying them with the towel that was wrapped around Him."* (John 13:1-4).

Now while John says nothing about the institution of the

25

Last Supper, this appears to be the same Passover Meal spoken about by the Synoptics. There is a further deliberate identifying of Jesus as the Passover Lamb by John in his crucifixion narrative, where he writes, *"When they came to Jesus and found that He was already dead. They did not break His legs.... These things happened so that the Scripture would be fulfilled: Not one of His bones will be broken"* (John 19:33,37). This is a direct quotation from the original Passover regulations (cf. Ex. 12:46).

Paul also interprets the Lord's Supper against the background of the Passover, when he writes, *"Get rid of the old yeast that you may be a new batch without yeast - as you really are. For Christ our Passover Lamb (pascha), has been sacrificed. Therefore, let us keep the Festival, not with the old yeast, the yeast of malice and wickedness, but with bread without yeast, the bread of sincerity and truth"* (1 Cor. 5:7-8; cf. Ex. 12:15 & 19).

Similarly, Peter, writing in his famous passage on Redemption, says, *"For you know that it was not with perishable things such as silver or gold that you were redeemed from the empty way of life handed down to you from your forefathers, but with the precious blood of Christ, a Lamb without blemish or defect."* (1 Pet. 1:18-19, cf. Ex. 12:5).

We find this same Paschal motif in the Apocalypse where Christ is hymned as the *"slain Lamb"*, *"who loves us and has freed us from our sins by his blood"* (Rev. 1:3, 5:6-9). The special significance of this last reference will be appreciated if we note that the word for 'slain' (*"cut the throat"*) in Revelation 5:6, *esphagmenon*, is the same one used in the instructions concerning the slaying of the Passover Lambs, in Exodus 12:6. It reads, (in the LXX version), *"all the people of the community of Israel must slaughter them - (sphaxousin - literally," cut the throat") at twilight:"* On the basis of these, as well as all those other New Testament references to the idea of redemption (so much a theme of the Exodus story) it is clear that the Early Church saw a connection between the Lord's Supper and the Passover.

The Passover Table

As we look at the Lord's Supper against the backdrop of the

Passover, it will be helpful at the outset, to consider the various items traditionally placed on the Seder table. Of course, we cannot be sure that the items found there today are the same as those on the table at the Last Supper. However, because of the Jews' scrupulous observance of their traditions, through the millennia, there will be similarities.

The two most important items on the table, for our present study, are the unleavened bread or *matzos* (as it is called) and the wine cup(s). There are usually three *matzos* biscuits or wafers, wrapped in an embroidered pouch, and ready to be used in a prescribed order. A wine glass is placed in front of each table setting, ready to be filled from a central decanter, at least four times during the meal. Each time the glass is filled it is called by a different name, to fit in with the various stages of the ceremony. The first cup is called "the cup of sanctification;" (sometimes, "the cup of consecration"); the second, "the cup of redemption;" the third, "the cup of blessing;" and the fourth, "the cup of praise."

Other items on the table include, a roasted or hard-boiled egg, small dishes of salt water (symbol of Israel's bitter tears in Egypt), a thick puree, called charoseth made from dates, chopped fruit and wine (symbolical of the mud used to make the bricks in Egypt), a dish of parsley, lettuce or celery (symbol of the hyssop); a dish of horse radish (symbol of the bitter herbs of the original Passover) (cf. Ex. 12:8), and usually, a roasted lamb shank bone. Besides these menu items, an extra place setting, complete with a goblet of wine, as well as vacant chair, will all be set "for Elijah". The Jews expect that Messiah will come at Passover season and will be introduced by Elijah. So much for the Passover table.

The Actual Ceremony

Before the Passover commences the head of the house takes a candle and broom and makes a cursory, symbolical search of the house. His purpose is to ensure that no trace of leaven has been missed in the spring cleaning done prior to Passover season. This is the background of Paul's reference in 1 Corinthians 5:7-8.

Another interesting feature is the studied gesture of those who come to share in the meal. They recline with their left elbow on the table. This is to symbolize their being at ease and in full enjoyment of their freedom from the bondage of Egypt. Matthew actually notes, *"when evening came, Jesus was reclining (anekeitō) at the table with the Twelve"* (Matthew 26:20)

The Passover ceremony begins with the *kiddush*, or prayer of consecration "Blessed art Thou O Lord, our God, King of the Universe, Creator of the fruit of the vine". At this point the wine is poured and the "Cup of sanctification" is enjoyed. Several set procedures follow. First, there is a ceremonial hand washing before eating the parsley or lettuce that has already been dipped in salt water. Next comes the first "breaking of the bread". At this point, the head of the house takes the middle piece of the three matzos wafers, breaks it in two and distributes it among all present, saying, "This is the bread of affliction which our ancestors ate in the land of Egypt; let all those who are hungry, enter and eat thereof; and all who are in distress, come and celebrate the Passover."

Next comes the *Haggadah* ("proclamation") which is a rather lengthy and sometimes embellished telling of the story of the Exodus. The story is often told in response to a series of questions which are asked by the youngest person present (cf. Ex. 13:14).

Several other things take place before the actual meal. They are: the singing of the first part of the *Hallel* (Psalms 113-115); the second cup: the cup of Redemption; the sharing of more bitter herbs, the giving of the *sop* (a small sandwich made from two small pieces of matzos with a filling of charoseth) to a favored guest, and the saying of the following grace, "Blessed art thou, O Eternal our God, King of the Universe, who hast sanctified us with thy commandments and commanded us to eat unleavened bread."

The Passover meal itself is a hearty meal of roast lamb, with all the trimmings. It is eaten in leisurely fashion and in an atmosphere of festive celebration. Once everyone has had his fill, the meal concludes with the breaking and sharing of the remaining half of the middle matzos, which is called, the

Afikomen. Traditionally, after this no more food is eaten during the evening.

Following the meal a series of events completes the Passover ceremony. There are the third and fourth cups, the Cup of Blessing and the Cup of Praise, respectively. A series of prayers follow, as well as the singing of the rest of the *Hallel* - Psalms 116-118 and Psalm 136. The evening concludes with the expressed hope, "The following year grant us to be in Jerusalem!"

The preceding details show us how Jesus' actions and words at the Last Supper grew quite naturally out of the Passover meal. The *Afikomen* (the middle matzos) was in all likelihood, the "bread" which Jesus used to institute His Supper and about which He said, *"this is My body"*. This, no doubt, would have surprised His disciples who would have expected Him to say, in accordance with tradition, *"this is the bread of affliction which our fathers..."* (cf. Deut. 16:3). Incidentally, some Messianic Jewish commentators see a Trinitarian symbolism in the three Passover *matzos*, especially since Jesus took the middle piece to represent Himself, when He said, *"This is My body..."* Obviously, it was the third cup, the cup of blessing, that became the cup about which Jesus said, *"This is my blood of the covenant which is poured out for many, for the forgiveness of sins,"* (Matt. 26:28; cf. 1 Cor. 11:16).

Chapter 4

Festival Parallels

Living Memorial

As we look at some of the parallels between the Passover and the Lord's Supper, it is important to understand that the special purpose of the carefully orchestrated Passover ceremony is not only to assist in commemorating history but to actually share in it by recapturing the story of the Exodus, in a symbolic way. Thus, although shrouded in the mists of time, the details of Israel's deliverance from Egypt come alive for each new generation of Jews. As the Mishnah puts it, "In every generation a man must so regard himself as if he came forth himself out of Egypt."

So it is with the Lord's Supper. When Jesus said, *"do this in remembrance of Me"* He was not merely saying, "don't forget Me." He was in fact, urging the disciples, as well as all those believers who would follow after them, to participate, physically, emotionally and spiritually in a living remembrance. It is this that makes the Lord's Supper so special. We are not just remembering historical events but sharing in true fellowship with our Risen Lord. This remembrance of Jesus is not simply a recitation of facts but vital worship, as we realize afresh our deliverance from sin through His redeeming sacrifice. Israel's feast commemorates redemption from physical bondage. At the Lord's Supper we remember our Saviour who through His death on the cross, rescued us from sin's bondage and brought us into the blessing of eternal redemption. The bread of affliction and the bitter herbs give way to a participation in the bread and wine of blessing.

Reverent Informality

Another point of comparison between the Passover and the Lord's Supper is the atmosphere in which both are celebrated. The Passover is essentially a family and community experience, not an ecclesiastical or political ceremony. It is informal not liturgical. Even the slaying of the Paschal lambs in the original event, was the responsibility of the head of the household, not the priest (Ex. 12:3,6,21). Parents, children, neighbours and friends, providing they are members of the covenant community and not precluded on grounds of ritual defilement, participate together.

This too, was the setting of the Last Supper. Jesus reclined informally with His own followers, in the upper room of' a home. It is surely a parody of the Lord's Supper that wraps it in the esoteric idiom of ecclesiastical jargon and sees it as the peculiar province of a clerical elite. Such ideas are as foreign to the Lord's Supper, just as they were to the Passover.

There was a remarkable inclusiveness about the Passover. Everyone in the family had a place at the Paschal table. The only people excluded were uncircumcised foreigners (Ex. 12:43-49) and Israelites who had contracted ritual defilement. Even in this latter case provision was made for them in the "water of separation"—a ceremonial mixture of running water and the ashes of a red heifer (cf. Numbers 19).

Moral Purity

In Bible times, a special supply of "heifer ashes" was kept in the environs of Jerusalem. Any pilgrim attending Passover who ran into unexpected defilement, such as walking across an unmarked grave or touching a carcass, could avail himself of cleansing. Once cleansed, he could attend a second celebration one month later (cf. Num. 9:6-11). This is the kind of situation envisaged in John 11:55. Other references to this cleansing from ritual defilement are found in Hebrews 9:13 and 10:22.

This is all very instructive as far as the Lord's Supper is concerned. All true believers are encouraged to be present and to see to it that they are in a cleansed condition of both heart and mind. Sin is to be judged, not used as an excuse for absentee-ism. As Paul puts it, *"let a man examine himself and so let him eat"* (1 Cor. 11:28). There is no spiritual defilement that, once con-fessed, cannot be cleansed by the precious blood of Christ (cf.1 John 1:7-9). As noted earlier, the apostle makes this point again, in 1 Cor. 5:7-8. He is saying that just as the Jews were fastidious about making sure their houses were free of leaven, in order to be ceremonially clean prior to their celebration of the Passover, so Christians should be concerned about moral purity as they approach the Lord's Table.

Paul is even more specific and searching in 1 Corinthians 11:28-29, *"Therefore whoever eats the bread or drinks the cup of the Lord, in an unworthy manner will be guilty of sinning against the body and blood of the Lord. A man ought to examine himself before he eats of the bread and drinks of the cup. For anyone who eats and drinks without recognizing the body of the Lord, eats and drinks judgment on himself."* More than likely, the apostle has the solemn words of Numbers 19:20 in mind: *"But if a person who is unclean does not purify himself he must be cut off from the community because he has defiled the sanctuary of the Lord. The water of cleansing is not on him and he is unclean."* (cf. 1 Cor. 3:16-17).

Of course, Paul's words in 1 Corinthians 11:28-29 had a par-ticular, local application for the church at Corinth. By practi-cing social discrimination in their meetings for the breaking of bread, they were failing to discern the body. That is, they were failing to give due, practical recognition to the truth of the one-ness of the mystical Body of Christ, the Church. Secondly, by associating with pagan rituals they were failing to recognize the distinctiveness and sanctity of the local assembly. This is the point of Paul's further admonition in 1 Corinthians 10:21, *"You cannot drink the cup of the Lord and the cup of demons too."*

Community Involvement

Another parallel between the Passover and the Lord's Supper is the involvement of the covenant community. For example, in Exodus 12:6 we read, *"all the people of the commun-ity (Qahal; regularly translated ekklēsia in LXX) of Israel must slaughter them (i.e. Paschal lambs) at twilight"*. Then, in verse 47, a further caveat is added, *"The whole community of Israel must celebrate it"* (i.e. the Passover).

The New Testament lays similar emphasis on the importance of corporate Christian worship. For example, in Hebrews 10:24-25 in the context where he speaks about the importance of *"having our hearts sprinkled from an evil conscience and our bodies washed with pure water,"* (an obvious reference to Numbers 19), the writer goes on to say, *"let us consider one another to provoke unto love and good works; not forsaking the assembling of ourselves together as the manner of some is,"* (see also, Ps. 22:22 and Heb. 2:12; Deut. 23:2 and Acts 7:38). Deliberate absence from the Passover was a serious matter in Israel. Should we Christians be any less concerned about absenting ourselves from the Lord's Supper? (cf. Ex. 12:6; Num. 19:20).

Feast of Redemption

The Jews call the Passover, "the season of our freedom" and, the "Feast of Redemption". Whatever traditions were added later, this festival above all else, commemorated Israel's deliverance from Egypt. The Old Testament regularly views this deliverance as a redemptive act of God (Ex. 6:6; 15:13; Deut. 7:8; 13:5; 1 Chron. 17:21). This particular point was specially memorialized in the ritual consecration and redemption of the firstborn of both man and beast (Ex. 12:11-16, Lev. 27:26, cf. Luke 2:23). Significantly, according to tradition, the boring of the ear of the "perpetual slave" took place at Passover time (cf. Exodus 21:5-6; Psalm 40:6).

Just as Israel's redemption was sealed by the shed blood of the Paschal lamb, so, as believers, we are *"redeemed by the precious blood of Christ"* (1 Pet. 1:19; Eph. 1:7; Mark 10:45). This is recalled in our Lord's words of institution. *"This cup is the new covenant in My blood, which is poured out for (huper) you"* (Luke 2:20). His point is unmistakable. In Egypt, it was the sprinkled blood of the lamb that spoke of redemption. It also symbolized their being brought into a covenant relationship with Jehovah. Similarly, it is the redeeming blood of Christ that we remember as we share the memorial cup. Every time we partake of the Lord's Supper we are reminded of our redemption from sin and challenged to reconsecrate ourselves as Christ's willing servants.

Looking Forward

Another spiritual parallel between the Passover and the Lord's Supper is worth noting: both are forward-looking. The original Passover not only anticipated the imminent deliverance and departure of Israel from Egypt by the almighty hand of Jehovah, but also their journey to the Promised Land. It was truly a new beginning – "the beginning of months." Their clothing as well as their calendar indicated their preparedness to move forward into a future of blessing with God (Ex. 12:11). To this day, this anticipative aspect of Passover is not forgotten, as we have already seen. Not only is the place set for Elijah, but at one point in the Passover proceedings someone, usually a child, will go to and open the door to see if Elijah has indeed arrived, ready to introduce Messiah! Then, as the Passover supper ends, that age-long hope is expressed, "next year in Jerusalem."

Surely this forward-look is an essential aspect of the Christian celebration of the Lord's Supper. As Paul writes, *"for whenever you eat this bread and drink this cup, you proclaim the Lord's death until He comes"* (1 Cor. 11:26). In the Lord's Supper we not only proclaim our faith in Christ's Person and redeeming death, but in His Glorious Advent. The Supper is like a bridge linking the First and Second Advents. One elder I knew, used to place an empty chair at the communion table, not only to stimulate our hope but to make the point that our Coming Lord was present among us by His Spirit.

So we see that while the Passover meal and The Lord's Supper belong to two diverse traditions and are as different in their symbolism as the faiths they represent, they have parallel features. We shall better understand the significance of our Christian festival of remembrance if, like the New Testament writers, we view it against the background of the Jewish festival. If Passover season is a time of joyous celebration among Jews, how much more ought we to rejoice in remembering our

Saviour. He who died for us and rose again now lives as our Great High Priest and is coming soon. Let us never allow morbid traditions to rob us of our birthright of joy and hope.

Part 2

The Teaching of Jesus and the Apostle Paul

"Our Lord Jesus Christ hath knit together a company of new people by sacraments, most few in number, most easy to be kept, most excellent in signification." Augustine of Hippo (A.D. 354 – 430.)

Chapter 5

Jesus Institutes His Supper

Parallel accounts of the Institution of the Lord's Supper

1 Cor. 11:23-26	Matt. 26:26-30	Mark 14:22-26	Luke 22:19-20
For I received from the Lord what I also passed on to you:			But the hand of him who is going to betray Me is with Mine on the table
The Lord Jesus, on the night He was betrayed	While they were eating	While they were eating	
took bread, and when he had given thanks He broke it and said,	Jesus took bread, gave thanks and broke it,	Jesus took bread, gave thanks and broke it,	And He took the bread, gave thanks, broke it
"This is My body, which is for you; do this in remembrance of Me."	and gave it to His disciples saying, "take and eat; this is my body."	and gave it to His disciples saying, "take it; this is My body."	and gave it to them saying, "This is My body for you; do this in remembrance of Me."
In the same way, after supper He took the cup, saying,	Then He took the cup, gave thanks and offered it to them, saying,	Then He took the cup, gave thanks and offered it to them, and they all drank from it	In the same way after the supper He took the cup, saying,

1 Cor. 11:23-26	Matt. 26:26-30	Mark 14:22-26	Luke 22:19-20
"This cup is the new covenant in My blood;"	"Drink from it, all of you. This is My blood of the covenant,"	"This is My blood of the covenant,"	"This cup is the new covenant in My blood,"
	which is poured out for many for the forgiveness of sins	which is poured out for many, He said to them	which is poured out for you
do this, whenever you drink it in remembrance of Me			
	"I tell you, I will not drink of this fruit of the vine from now on until that day when I drink it anew with you in My Father's kingdom."	"I tell you the truth, I will not drink again of the fruit of the vine until that day when I drink it anew in the kingdom of God."	"For I tell you, I will not drink of the fruit of the vine until the kingdom of God comes."
	When they had sung a hymn, they went out to the Mount of Olives.	When they had sung a hymn, they went out to the Mount of Olives.	

The Emblems

A careful reading of the foregoing, parallel records of our Lord's words of institution reveals several interesting comparisons. Before looking at these in more detail, it will be helpful to note that where our English versions refer to bread (*artos*) or loaf, it is the unleavened bread (*matzos*) of the Passover meal that is in view. This biscuit or "cracker" as we might describe it, was passed from hand to hand with each person breaking off a piece and eating it.

On a personal note, I remember breaking bread with a group

of Christians at Tiberias in Galilee, one hot summer's day. We used matzos and Passover wine, which had been graciously provided by a friendly, local rabbi. There was something rather special about the actual passing and breaking of the matzos biscuit. Even the sound, as each believer broke off his portion, seemed to emphasize the symbolism and realism of the occasion.

Although Jesus makes no reference to wine but simply to this cup, it is clear that there was wine in the cup and that each disciple was invited to drink from it. Clearly the cup was the "cup of blessing," the third cup of the Passover meal (cf. 1 Cor. 10:16). We note that Jesus said that He would not drink of the *"fruit of the vine"* until He drank it "new" in the kingdom of God. Once again, His words seem to echo the ancient prayer still spoken at the Passover table, "Blessed art thou O Lord our God, King of the Universe, Creator of the fruit of the vine".

About The Bread

Paul's account in 1 Corinthians 11, the earliest written record, is almost identical with that of the Synoptists, regarding the bread. Three details are noted in all the accounts: *"Jesus took bread, He broke bread and said, 'this is My body'"*. The following, slight variations are worth noting. Matthew and Mark record Jesus' invitation to, *"take"* Matthew adds, *"eat"* Luke adds after, *"My body"*, the words, *"which is given for you"*. While Paul adds (in some mss.) *"which is broken for you."* Luke and Paul add: *"do this in remembrance of Me"*. Matthew and Mark add, *eulogēsas* (literally, "blessed") (cf. 1 Cor. 10:16). Luke and Paul add: *eucharistēsas* (literally, *"gave thanks"*).

About The Cup

There are two features common to all four records, concerning the cup. First, the words, *"He took the cup,"* (the definite article is omitted by Mark and also from some mss. of Matthew.) Second, Jesus' saying, *"My blood of the new covenant"* (some mss. omit "new" from Matthew and Mark). Other textual variations include:

i.   in Matthew and Mark *"gave thanks and offered it to them"*.

ii.   Luke and Paul include a note regarding the timing of the cup and tell us that Jesus took it *"after supper"*

iii.   Matthew alone records Jesus' words, *"drink ye all from it"*.

iv.   Paul alone records the words, *"do this, whenever you drink it, in remembrance of Me"*.

v.   Mark says, *"They all drank from it"*.

vi.   Matthew and Mark record Jesus' words, *"poured out for many"* while Luke uses the more personal, *"poured out for you"*.

vii.   Matthew adds: *"for the forgiveness of sins"*.

It is worth noting, in passing, that despite the various controversies, such as whether the wine is changed into the blood of Jesus; whether the pouring out of the wine is symbolical of the shedding of Christ's blood; whether we should use fermented or unfermented wine; or, whether the cup should be denied the laity—the fact remains that, nowhere in the New Testament is wine actually said to be a symbol of the blood of the Saviour. The word used regularly in those passages that deal with the Lord's supper, is "cup". This should surely alert us to the dangers of dogmatism regarding eucharistic practices and warn against interpretive addenda.

Another point worth noting is this: in 1 Corinthians 10:16 Paul speaks of the *"cup of blessing which we bless"* (KJV). In some ecclesiastical circles this has given rise to the idea of the so-called, "consecration of the cup". However, such a suggestion is surely alien to Paul's thought. He is simply recognizing that Jesus used the regular description of the third Passover cup. For a Jew this meant, *"the cup for which we bless or praise God"* (cf. NIV). Remember the prayer of consecration spoken at the outset of the Passover meal, "blessed art Thou O Lord, Our God…".

Attempting A Harmony

The following is a suggested conflation of the four institution narratives:

> "The Lord Jesus on the night He was betrayed, while they were eating, took bread and when He had given thanks, He broke it and gave it to His disciples. He said, 'Take and eat, this is My body which is given for you; do this in remembrance of Me.' In the same way, after supper, He took the cup, gave thanks and offered it to them, saying, 'This cup is the new covenant in my blood which is poured out for many, for the forgiveness of sins: drink from it all of you' (and they all drank from it). 'Do this whenever you drink it in remembrance of Me. I tell you the truth, I will not drink again of the fruit of the vine until that day when I drink it anew in the kingdom of God.'"

Generally, Matthew tends to agree with Mark, as Luke does with Paul. Matthew and Mark both omit the phrase, *"do this in remembrance of Me"*, while Luke and Paul include it. Then, while all three Synoptists include the pouring out of the covenant blood, and Jesus' declining to drink the fruit of the vine until the coming of the Kingdom, Paul omits these details. However, the apostle does include a reference to the Lord's Coming and mentions that the Supper was instituted by Jesus on the night of His betrayal. If there is a difference of emphasis between the Synoptics and Paul, it is that while the former is narrative, the latter tends to be didactic.

The Timing

There is considerable discussion regarding the timing of the Last Supper. This is occasioned by the fact that the Synoptic Gospels appear to follow a different time-table from John. Although a detailed examination of this issue lies outside the purpose of this book, it is worth a brief comment. The Synoptists picture Jesus instituting His Supper, prior to His arrest and during the course of a regular Jewish Passover meal. Such a meal would normally be held on the evening of the fourteenth of *Nisan* (or *Abib* – to use its earlier name). Mark is quite specific: *"On the first day of the Feast of Unleavened Bread, when it was customary to sacrifice the Passover Lamb, Jesus' disciples asked Him, 'Where do You want us to go and make preparations for You to eat the Passover?'"* (see Mark 14:12 cf. Matt. 26:17-19; Luke 22:7-23 and Ex. 12:1-6).

Although nothing is mentioned about it in connection with the meal Jesus shared with His disciples, normally, the featured item on the table would be the roast flesh of a lamb slain earlier in the day. John however, appears to have a different time in mind, judging from the following. In his description of Jesus' trial before the Roman governor, John writes, *"Then the Jews led Jesus from Caiaphas to the palace of the Roman governor. By now it was early morning, and to avoid ceremonial uncleanness, the Jews did not enter the palace; they wanted to be able to eat the Passover"* (John 18:28).

From this it appears that John is still anticipating the Passover. Second, he tells us that Jesus' trial and subsequent execution, took place on *"the day of Preparation of Passover week,"* (19:14) - which would be Friday. The term *paraskeuē* ("preparation") was the regular Jewish term for the day before their weekly Sabbath. Consistent with this, John mentions further that this particular Sabbath was, *megalē hē hēmera* ("the great day"; KJV *"high day"*; NIV *"a special Sabbath"*) in verse 31. Third, as noted earlier, the fourth evangelist points out that the death of Jesus was the literal fulfillment of the slaying of the Passover lamb. He writes: *"But when they came to Jesus and found that He was already dead, they did not break His legs.... These things happened so that the scriptures would be fulfilled: 'Not one of His bones will be broken.'"* (19:36 cf. Ex. 12:46).

Various attempts have been made to harmonize the accounts but none is altogether satisfactory. We shall be wise to refrain from dogmatism until we have more information. Much of the difficulty would be resolved if it could be demonstrated that the meal in John 13 was the Passover, the Last Supper of the Synoptics. This may not be as problematic as it appears on the surface. For example, the King James Version rendering of John 13:1, *"Now before the feast of the Passover, when Jesus knew that His hour was come...."* is not the only one possible. We could just as correctly read with the AMPL (et al.), *"Before the Paschal feast began, Jesus already knew that the time had come...."* In other words, John is not necessarily differentiating between two feasts. He is simply emphasizing Jesus' foreknowledge of the events about to take place. In spite of that knowledge, He proceeds to celebrate the Passover with His disciples.

In confirmation of this view we note that several traditional Passover practices are mentioned in John 13. For example, there is the ceremonial washing (feet, rather than hands) v.5; the giving of the sop to an honored guest, v. 26; the participants' reclining posture, v.12; and the suggestion about giving money to the poor, v.29. True, the mention of buying supplies for the feast (v. 29), presents something of a problem, unless of course it relates to buying things for the rest of the festive week rather than just the actual Passover meal. In any case, John says this was only a thought that occurred to some of the disciples; Jesus gave no actual instructions. Coming back to the difficulty presented by John 18:28 with its suggestion that the Passover was still ahead. One resolution of this might be to read, *to pascha* as referring not to the actual Passover itself but to the ensuing Feast of Unleavened Bread. Admittedly, this is unlikely, but it is feasible and has many scholarly advocates.

Finally, John's citing of Exodus 12:46 (cf. John 19:36) in fact, has little bearing on chronology. He is simply reminding his readers that Jesus would die as *"the Lamb of God who bears away the sin of the world"* (cf. John 1:29,36). For John, who had a special interest in details, the fact that none of Jesus' bones were broken (only those of the malefactors) was one more sign that the Lord really was God's redeeming Paschal Lamb. In this, John would be in agreement with Paul who also saw Christ as, *"our Passover Lamb"* (1 Cor. 5:7). By the way, Paul saw no conflict between such an interpretation and the Synoptic time-table, as we see from his statement, *"The Lord Jesus, on the night He was betrayed, took bread...."* (1 Cor. 11:23).

While, as observed, we may be unable to reach a final conclusion about the difference between the Synoptists and John, one thing seems clear. Jesus deliberately chose to eat His special Passover meal with His disciples one day earlier than the official day, according to Jewish reckoning (Luke 22:15-16). This should not be considered unusual since as scholars tell us, there is evidence for a variety of Passover dates even among Jews. For example, there was evidently such a calendrical dispute between the Pharisees and the Sadducees. Furthermore, the Dead Sea Scrolls show that in the Essene community at Qumran a different calendar date was observed for Passover. In any case just as Jesus is the "Lord of the Sabbath," so He is Lord and fulfillment of the Passover. He can as easily celebrate it when He chooses as He can set it aside as no longer relevant. Perhaps here lies the solution. The New Testament writers are more concerned to describe the Lord's Supper and its meaning, than to satisfy chronological speculation.

Before we move on, one thing should be carefully noted: it is the point Paul makes, that Jesus instituted His memorial supper, *"in the night in which He was betrayed"*. Amazingly, especially in light of the Lord's foreknowledge of all that lay ahead of Him, He was thinking more about His disciples than Himself. This of course is so evident in the Upper Room Discourse (John 13-16). Jesus is more anxious to console and show friendship to His followers than to seek sympathy for Himself. Certainly He wanted them to remember him, but this was because He knew that in that very remembrance they would find hope and strength to carry on through the dark days ahead.

The Place

We discover from Luke's account that Jesus had made careful plans to enjoy the Passover celebration with His disciples. He not only sent Peter and John to find and prepare the room, but had gone to some lengths to conceal its location. This may well have been to forestall any attempt by Judas to betray Jesus prematurely. Furthermore, we notice that Jesus had pre-arranged both the use of the Upper Room and the signal which would

direct Peter and John to it. It is clear that Jesus had willing help-
ers and disciples who, although remaining anonymous, were
happy to do whatever they could to assist, for example *"a man
bearing a pitcher of water"*.

We note that the place Jesus selected for His Supper, is
described as the 'guest chamber' (*kataluma*) (Mark 14:14; Luke
22:11). The only other New Testament reference to a *kataluma* is
in Luke's nativity story, where it is usually translated, 'inn' (cf.
Luke 2:7). A literal translation of the word would be, 'a place
of unyoking' or 'unburdening.' It is surely significant that the
Saviour, for whom there was no *"place to lay His head,"* let alone
unburden His heart, prepared such a place for His own. What
is more, He did so just before going on to the cross where He
would lift the burden of our sins forever.[2]

---

2   For a careful and scholarly discussion of the matters we have considered in
    this chapter, the reader is referred to: Leon Morris, *The Gospel according to John*
    (NICNT) pp. 774-786; Norval Guldenhuy's, *Commentary on the Gospel of Luke*
    (NICNT) pp. 550-560 & I. Howard Marshall's *Last Supper and Lord's Supper*,
    Paternoster Press p. 72

Chapter 6

What Did Jesus Mean?

Having looked at the institution of the Lord's Supper in more general terms, we can now examine Jesus' actual words of institution. Here, we are more interested in understanding His meaning than in theological interpretations. That is to say, we will try to discern our Lord's words in their original, historical, cultural setting. After all, the best way to grasp the sense of scripture, and in particular the words of Jesus, is to ask what His words meant for His original hearers.

Only if we have some idea of the contemporary idiom and metaphor (aside from the nuances of words and phrases as we hear them) shall we feel the full impact of what is being said. There is always the danger of reading accepted meanings and modern interpretations back into scripture, and that can be quite misleading.

Two other observations are called for. First, the bread and wine sitting on the table in front of Jesus, already had their own symbolism as items for a Passover meal. The unleavened bread in particular, had a double significance. On the one hand, it recalled an historical drama; the fact that the fleeing Israelites had no time to wait for their bread to rise or leaven. On the other hand, it symbolized Israel's religious and moral concern to be cleansed and separated from all that was evil (see Ex. 12:8,15,20; 13:3,7-8; Deut. 16;3-4). Leaven evidently had a very negative connotation for them.

Second, there appears to have been a considerable interval between Jesus' words concerning the bread and those concerning the cup. In fact, according to Luke's phrase, *"after the Supper"* (*meta to deipnēsai*), the whole Passover Seder intervened (Luke 22:20). All this suggests an informal, family-like setting and certainly an absence of liturgical or ceremonial intent. It is noteworthy that while inviting His disciples to drink from the cup, Jesus Himself declined to do so, for His own stated reasons. It is sometimes suggested that the cup Jesus declined to drink was the fourth Passover cup rather than, "the cup of blessing" (cf. Luke.22:4-18).

Since our understanding of the Lord's Supper will depend very largely on our explanation of these central words of Jesus, we must examine them carefully while trying to step back into the scene in the Upper Room. Presumably, Jesus and His disciples had spread a traditional Jewish Passover table, just like Jewish families had done across the centuries. As we have seen, among other items on the table there would be unleavened biscuits and cups of wine — each having its own particular name and significance, in keeping with Jewish tradition.

Jesus now reaches out His hand (part of His physical body), takes a piece of the unleavened bread, gives thanks, breaks it and gives it to His disciples. As He does so, He says, "*take and eat, this is My body.*" In effect, He is saying to the disciples that whereas, until now, the unleavened bread has served as a memorial token of their forefathers' deliverance from Egypt, in future He wishes them to think of it as a reminder of Himself and His redeeming work.

It will certainly help us understand Jesus' meaning if we again recall the words spoken at a Passover meal by the celebrant, usually the father as head of the household: "*This is the bread of affliction which our fathers ate when they came out of Egypt*" (cf. Deut. 16:3). No one sitting at the table would think the father meant that this piece of *matzos* he was holding in his hand was the actual unleavened bread the Israelites ate at the time of the Exodus, all those centuries earlier! They would obviously understand him to mean that this bread represented the original unleavened cakes that fed the Israelites on their desert trek.

Theological opinions aside, surely what the disciples understood Jesus to mean when He said, "*This is My body,*" was that the bread they saw Him holding in His hand, simply represented His body. It would not have occurred to them that He was saying that by some mysterious alchemy the bread had been changed into His physical body! That would have seemed quite bizarre to them. Obviously, they would not have thought in terms of two bodies, the one holding the bread and the other, the bread Jesus held.

Jesus' disciples were quite used to His speaking figuratively and metaphorically about Himself. It would not have occurred to them that He meant that the unleavened bread was now His physical flesh anymore than they would have thought of Him as a literal door, or vine, or loaf of bread (cf. John 6,10 & 15). Furthermore, we see that Jesus used the verb 'to be' with the meaning 'represents' elsewhere in His teaching. For example, in His interpretation of the famous parable of the Sower He says: *"The seed is the word of God"* (Luke 8:11). Similarly, when explaining the Parable of the Tares He says, *"the field is the world"* (Matt. 13:38, cf. Gal. 4:24). Here in His words of institution, Jesus is simply offering a dramatic parable concerning His death, which was imminent. In this He is like the Old Testament prophets who often made their point, not just in words but in symbolic acts (cf. Jer. 13:2ff; 27:2). Jesus' words about the cup, *"this is My blood,"* would have been understood in the same way.

A couple of other points might be made here. First, in His words of Institution, Jesus consistently used the word *sōma* ('body') rather than *sarx* ('flesh'). This should warn us against a sacramental interpretation of words found in His "Bread of Life" discourse, often mistakenly related to the Lord's Supper even in some evangelical circles. In that allegory Jesus is clearly speaking figuratively but forcefully about receiving Him by faith, as the Incarnate Redeemer; the source and sustainer of spiritual life. He is not discussing *"the communion"* (cf. John 6:35, 53-56). This is particularly evident from His own explanation in verse 63, *"The Spirit gives life; the flesh counts for nothing. The words I have spoken to you are spirit and they are life."* (John 6:63).

It is particularly unfortunate that Jesus' symbolical words

about *"eating His flesh"* and *"drinking His blood"* have been taken out of context and used to support the unscriptural doctrine of transubstantiation. Such a materialistic interpretation of the Lord's words is a complete denial of biblical soteriology (the doctrine of salvation). We are not saved by taking the bread and wine at a communion service but by true faith in the saving, all-sufficient sacrifice of Christ at Calvary. Participation in the Lord's Supper is certainly no guarantee of salvation. Indeed, as Paul reminds the Corinthians, such superstitious ideas may be dangerous in the extreme.

Howard Marshall, writes,

> "The word is, which would have been absent from an original saying in Hebrew or Aramaic, can mean 'signify' as well as 'be identical with', and there can be no doubt whatever that at the Last Supper the word was used with the former meaning. The saying was uttered by Jesus while He was bodily present with the disciples and they could see His body and the bread were two separate things. "[3]

"Do This In Remembrance Of Me"

In these words, Jesus emphasizes the memorial aspect of this Supper. He is saying in effect that, just as The Passover commemorated Israel's deliverance from physical bondage in Egypt in Moses' day, so, in days to come, His Supper, "the Lord's Supper", as we know it, - would serve as a memorial of Himself, the One who delivers His people from spiritual bondage. Of course, there is also a contrast here too. Whereas the Passover commemorated an historical event, the Lord's Supper celebrates our living Lord. Jesus intended it to be a living remembrance – (*anamnēsis*), not just a wake! This is clear from Jesus' present imperative *"do (poi-eite) this continually for (eis) a remembrance of Me."* Incidentally, His use of the verb *poiein* does not carry even the slightest hint of 'making a sacrifice', as some mischievously suggest.

---

[3]   I Howard Marshall , *Last Supper and Lord's Supper* pp, 85-86.

"This Cup Is The New Covenant In My Blood Which Is Shed For Many For The Forgiveness Of Sins."

At least three important truths surface from these words of Jesus. First, there is the ratifying of a covenant relationship; second, the vicarious nature of His death; and third, the reality of forgiveness. Let us consider these.

(a) The New Covenant (*hē kainē diathēkē*)

As we have seen, all four Institution accounts include these words. Matthew and Mark read, *"My blood of the covenant"*; while Luke and Paul read, *"this cup is the new covenant in My blood"*. While various Old Testament covenants may be in view here, Jesus words are particularly reminiscent of those spoken by Moses at Sinai.

On that historic occasion, having assembled the Israelites, Moses first warns them against making covenants with the Canaanites and their gods (Ex. 23:32); then proceeds to explain the conditions of a covenant relationship with Jehovah. He then takes a basin of sacrificial blood, sprinkles half of it on the altar and half on the people. While doing so He says, "Behold the blood of the covenant, which the Lord hath made with you concerning all these words (margin: upon all these conditions) (Ex. 24:8; cf. Heb. 9:19-20).

In the light of this story we begin to see the significance of Jesus' own words. He is reminding His followers that just as Jehovah and Israel stood in a blood-sealed covenant relationship (a fact further illustrated in the Passover), so they and all who are His disciples, would enjoy a unique bond of relationship with Himself, sealed by His sacrifice at Calvary. The cup speaks of His own blood, *"the blood of the New Covenant"*. This Covenant unlike the Old, will not fail because of unfaithfulness on the part of one of the subscribing parties. The New Covenant depends solely on the saving sacrifice of one party, namely, the Lord Himself.

Let us not forget the solemnity of the occasion. While at the Supper that evening it was a symbolic cup of wine, next day it would be Jesus' own precious blood. In future, every time the followers of Jesus come together to share the memorial cup ideally they will be restating their commitment to Him and to the love covenant sealed by His precious blood. They will be confessing their oneness as Christ's "new-covenant congregation" and gratefully remembering His sacrifice on their behalf. The word translated 'covenant' here is *diathēkē*, which can also mean, 'a will' or 'testament' (see Heb. 9:16-17). This suggests that every time we *"drink from the cup"* we rejoice in all the blessings that are ours as Jesus' undeserving joint-heirs and beneficiaries.

(b) Vicarious Suffering

Matthew and Mark both report Jesus' saying, *"This is my blood of the covenant which is poured out for many"* (*peri pollōn*) (Matt. 26:28; Mark 14:24). Luke has *"This cup is the new covenant in My blood which is poured out for you"* (*huper humōn*). Although the wording is slightly different, the emphasis is the same. Jesus is saying that the cup commemorates His vicarious sacrifice - the shedding of His blood on behalf of sinners. The two different prepositions used in the foregoing phrases: *huper* and *peri* can both be translated 'on account of' or 'on behalf of', and are often used interchangeably. Of the two, *huper* is used more frequently in connection with the Lord's death for us sinners (see John 10:15; Acts 21:13; Rom. 5:6,8; 2 Cor. 5:21).

With this in mind, it is clear that when Jesus spoke His words of institution, particularly with reference to the cup, He intended His disciples to understand that it was to be a memorial of both His Glorious Person and His vicarious death. Every time they shared the cup, it would remind them that the Saviour not only died because of their sin, but, so that their sins could be forgiven. It is not too much to say, on the basis of Jesus' words, that whenever we celebrate the Lord's Supper we are saying "Jesus died instead of me." Here in essence, is a specific reference to the vicarious, atoning work of Christ. Having said that however, we should be careful not to impose our theological interpretation on Jesus' words. For example, when He says, *"poured out for many,"* He is not implying, "but not for all" as some would read it (cf. Matt. 20:28, I Tim. 2:6, Rom. 5:18-19).

Matthew includes Jesus' further statement, *"for the remission of sins"* (Matt. 26:28). His word 'remission' (*aphesin*) suggests the ideas of pardon, canceling of debt, quashing of sentence, and removal of penalty. Jesus is saying that His sacrifice effects the absolute removal of the due penalty of our sins. We drink the memorial cup and remind ourselves just how complete our deliverance really is. We affirm that though bankrupt spiritually, our debt is discharged absolutely. Though unquestionably guilty, we are declared unconditionally pardoned. We hear echoes of words from the great Servant Song, *"He was numbered with the transgressors and bore the sin of many"* (Isa. 53:12).

As we conclude this chapter, we reiterate an important truth: Jesus nowhere suggests that there is any saving efficacy resulting from our participation in His Supper. Such teaching makes a mockery of the Lord's Supper and is a blatant denial of what the Bible tells us about the finished work of Christ. Our remembrance of Christ has significance and spiritual value in that it focuses our thoughts on the Lord and His saving sacrifice. Bonar's famous communion hymn expresses it beautifully:

"Here, O my Lord, I see Thee face to face;
  Here faith can touch and handle things unseen;
  Here would I grasp with firmer hand Thy grace,
  And all my weariness upon Thee lean."

Horatius Bonar (1805-1889)

Chapter 7

Paul's Perspective

Paul's distinctive teaching concerning the Lord's Supper (sometimes called "the Pauline Eucharist") is found in his first Epistle to the Corinthians. Here are the three relevant passages:

i. *"Your boasting is not good. Don't you know that a little yeast works through the whole batch of dough? Get rid of the old yeast that you may be a new batch without yeast - as you really are. For Christ, our Passover lamb, has been sacrificed. Therefore let us keep the Festival, not with the old yeast, the yeast of malice and wickedness, but with bread without yeast, the bread of sincerity and truth."* (1 Cor. 5:6-8).

ii. *"Is not the cup of thanksgiving for which we give thanks a participation (koinōnia) in the blood of Christ? And is not the bread that we break a participation in the body of Christ? Because there is one loaf, we, who are many, are one body, for we all partake of the one loaf. You cannot drink the cup of the Lord and the cup of demons too; you cannot have a part in, both the Lord's table and the table of demons"* (1 Cor. 10:16-17,21).

iii. *"For I received (parelabon: "to receive from another") from the Lord what I also passed on (paredōka: "to commit") to you.... For whenever you eat this bread and drink this cup, you proclaim (katangellete) the Lord's death until He comes.... Therefore whoever eats the bread or drinks the cup of the Lord in an unworthy manner will be guilty of sinning against the body and blood of the Lord. A man ought to examine himself before he eats of' the bread and drinks of the cup. For anyone who eats and drinks without recognizing the body of the Lord eats and drinks judgment on himself "* (1 Cor. 11:23-29).

These passages which, of course, are without parallel in other

New Testament epistles, represent our earliest written sources concerning the Lord's Supper. Although the apostle includes the words of institution, he is particularly concerned here, with the on-going celebration of the Supper. In order to appreciate his teaching we must consider the context and circumstances out of which it grew. In 1 Corinthians Paul is answering specific questions posed by his readers. At the same time, he is seeking to straighten out various practical problems that have developed in the church at Corinth. Having said that, we see that there are timeless, universal principles enshrined in his teaching, including that regarding the Lord's Supper.

To a large degree, the problems in the church at Corinth mirrored the moral, social and cultural problems of the city itself. Diverse in the extreme, Corinth has been called, the "Vanity Fair of the Ancient World". Apart from its ethnic and cultural mix, it was a proud, cosmopolitan, maritime city of Greece. Snobbishness as well as blatant immorality flourished there. The social elite despised the common people (*hoi polloi*).

Paul saw that there were all kinds of factions and personality cults in the church. Two things that specially grieved him were, their flippant attitude toward moral issues and their cliquishness, evident even at the Lord's Supper. As far as he was concerned their meetings did *"more harm than good"* (v. 17). It seems that the "in crowd" who were fortunate enough to enjoy social freedom, were taking advantage of their less fortunate brothers and sisters, most of whom were slaves. They would arrive early for the *Agapē* or "Love Feast" — a communal meal associated with the Lord's Supper - and through their intemperance, turn the thing into something akin to an orgy. Then, when the poorer Christians arrived, having been delayed by their duties, they found themselves obliged to go hungry. Paul condemned such conduct as a denial of meaningful participation in the Lord's Supper: a failure *"to discern the Lord's Body."*

We may ask the question, "Why doesn't Paul write on the subject of the Lord's Supper in his other epistles?" Possibly because its regular celebration was already firmly established among other New Testament churches and conducted with

Christian propriety. He could, so to speak, take it for granted. His particular discussion of the subject in 1 Corinthians, as noted, was intended to rectify something which had gone terribly wrong. Incidentally, the omission of references to the Supper in Paul's other letters, in no way detracts from its importance nor suggests failure on the part of the early churches to observe it regularly (cf. Acts 2:42,46; 20:7). Furthermore, it is significant that, despite the variety of traditions and modes of celebration, the Lord's Supper has been a common and important feature of life in all Christian churches for two thousand years.

The third thing we note by way of introduction to Paul's teaching, is that there appears to be a close affinity between Luke's institution narrative and Paul's teaching. This is not surprising, since although the apostle had access to such original sources as Peter and John Mark, he spent considerable time with Luke, both in his travels and in his imprisonment. In fact, Paul's distinctive teaching regarding the Lord's Supper is really a matter of emphasis. He is in complete agreement with the Evangelists, Matthew and Mark and Luke, regarding the basic data. After all, we must remember that although 1 Corinthians is our earliest written source of information about the Supper, it does not predate the oral and apostolic traditions with which Paul would have been thoroughly familiar. Indeed, there would still be those living who had been present at The Last Supper with whom he could have spoken. Paul's words suggest that he had communicated his teaching to the Corinthians during his eighteen month stay in their city, A.D. 50-52.

Ethical Considerations

Having looked at the historical, political context we are now better able to examine Paul's particular emphases. Not surprisingly, the apostle is quite clear regarding the need for moral integrity in relation to the celebration of the Lord's Supper. Remember His words, *"Therefore, let us keep the festival not with the old yeast… but with… the bread of sincerity and truth"* (1 Cor. 5:7-8). Here, as suggested, Paul is looking at the Communion against the backdrop of the Jewish Passover. He implies that just as Christ is the antitype of the Paschal lamb, so the Lord's Supper, is a Christian fulfillment of the Feast of Unleavened Bread. Just as the Israelites were at pains to remove all leaven before keeping the Passover, so Christians should make sure their lives are clean before they celebrate the Lord's Supper. On the one hand, he tells his readers to be rid of "malice and wickedness" - his point being, we can only truly "keep the festival" or, as we would say, "remember the Lord," if we are willing to confess and deal with all known sin. On the other, he insists, *"...but with bread without yeast, the bread of sincerity and truth."* Thus he urges all who share the Lord's Supper to live lives of purity and positive goodness. We cannot divorce our participating in the Supper from Christian integrity. He mentions other moral prerequisites in 1 Corinthians 10:14,21,22, *"Therefore my dear friends, flee from idolatry... You cannot drink the cup of the Lord and the cup of demons too. You cannot have a part in both the Lord's table and the table of demons".*

Whereas in the preceding passage he has been speaking about personal morality, here he is challenging his readers to disassociate from social and public evils. He not only pleads for a clean break with idolatry but for separation from all involvement in the cultic orgies of the idol temples of Corinth. Participation in the pagan practice of *"eating of meat offered to idols"* (a problem he deals with in 1 Corinthians 8) was, for Paul, tantamount to "participating in demonism." He saw it as a matter of deliberate choice. Will his readers enjoy fellowship with Christ or with demons? The apostle says, in so many words, "you can't have it both ways!" He warns that to drink the *"cup of demons"* while at the same time drinking the *"cup of the Lord"* is to court spiritual disaster. In fact it will arouse the righteous jealousy of God!

In Paul's view, sharing in pagan sacrificial revelry no matter how it may be excused, is identifying with the whole system it represents. True, the idol may be a non-entity, the figment of fallen man's diseased imagination, but unfortunately, it can all too easily become a front for demonism. Involvement in pagan temple rites usually meant involvement in immoral practices. Hence his strident call for uncompromising separation from the pagan, religious systems of Corinth.

Paul's point in placing the cup and table of demons in conflict with the cup and table of the Lord is seen by some scholars as his repudiation of a superstitious attitude toward participating in communion. The suggestion is that the Corinthians were viewing the Lord's Supper as a sort of spiritual prophylactic. In other words, it was alright to participate in an idol festival as long as you took the precaution of attending the Lord's Supper afterwards: the one counteracted the other!

While the apostle's words relate particularly to Christians living in Corinth, a city immersed in pagan practices, his message is relevant for all times and places. To align ourselves with the social evils, moral perversions and religious pretensions of our contemporary society which, like that of Corinth, is masterminded by Satan, disqualifies us from fellowship with the Lord. That sounds uncompromising but that is the way Paul intended it to sound. We shall be wise not to dilute his teaching. As our Lord put it, we may be in the world but are not to be of it (cf. John 17:16-17).

While still on the subject of Communion and Christian ethics, Paul warns, "You Corinthians may come together for a communion service, but such are your attitudes toward each other that, whatever you may call your gathering, it is certainly not 'the Lord's Supper'" (cf. 1Cor.11:.20-21). What concerned him were the divisions in the assembly. He believed that these had such a deleterious effect on their celebration of the Lord's Supper, that people might just as well stay home! (cf. v. 17-18).

For the apostle, there could be no communion without genuine unity. In his view, the Corinthians' failure to wait for each other and accept each other without prejudice, was having serious spiritual consequences. Paul sees such behaviour as, *"despising the Church of God; sinning against the body and blood of the Lord;"* and *"drinking judgment on themselves"* (vv. 22,27 and 29). Those are serious words! Let's face it, how I treat my brothers and sisters in Christ, choosing with whom to have fellowship or with whom not to have fellowship, has a real bearing on the value of my worship and grieves the Holy Spirit (cf. Eph. 4:4; 30-32).

Just what Paul means by, *"sinning against"* or *"profaning the body and blood of Christ"* is hard to say. He probably means that to deny by sinful conduct what I profess by my attendance at the Lord's Supper, is the same spiritually speaking as, *"trampling the Son of God underfoot"* and treating *"as an unholy thing the blood of the covenant that sanctifies"* (cf. Heb. 10:29).

Of course, whether the severe consequences Paul mentions are to be expected today, as in his day, is something of an open question. Some biblical interpreters believe that extreme physical judgements, such as those described in 1 Corinthians 11:30 and Acts 5, are not to be regarded so much as precedents, but as warnings to the first generation of Christians. They were living in the initial epoch of Christianity, the apostolic era, and nothing could be allowed to compromise those inaugural movements of the Spirit. However, surely we must be careful not to water down the seriousness of the nature or the consequences of sin among the people of God in any generation! (cf. 1 Cor. 16:22).

Finally, in this matter of ethics and the Lord's Supper, Paul urges self-examination, *"A man ought to examine himself before he eats of the bread and drinks of the cup"* (v. 28). Obviously, important and revealing though this exercise may be, it is intended to be remedial and restorative. The apostle is not counseling an unhealthy, unproductive introspection but rather a vigorous and honest confession of sin, so that we can maintain communion with the Lord and His people.

Chapter Eight

Communion and Remembrance

Communion

Another Pauline distinctive is his teaching about *"communion."* He writes, *"The cup of blessing which we bless, is it not the communion of the blood of Christ? The bread which we break, is it not the communion of the body of Christ?"* (1 Cor. 10:16 KJV). Although the apostle uses the term 'communion' here, in a eucharistic context, it would be a mistake to think of it in its developed, technical sense of "The Communion." He is not concerned with doctrinal or liturgical ideas so much, but with practical matters such as Christian unity and commitment.

As a matter of fact, Paul has an unusual order here: mentioning the cup before the bread. He is pointing out that when Christians celebrate the Lord's Supper, sharing in the cup and the bread, they are giving visible witness to their mutual participation in Christ and in the benefits of the Cross. He is not saying that they are receiving or sharing the body and blood of Christ, in some mystical or quasi-physical sense. He is speaking figuratively (as is obvious from verse 17) reminding his readers that their Christian fellowship is based on the incarnation and saving sacrifice of Christ. It is not a matter of the communication of grace but the communion of saints, secured by Christ Himself.

Communion, as often stated, is based on union and that surely is the point the apostle is making here. It would be especially important to remind the Corinthian believers of this since they seemed so prone to schism. Paul's metaphor is clear, *"For we being many are one bread (artos: 'loaf') and one body: for we are all partakers of that one bread (loaf)"* (1 Cor. 10:17). He is saying in effect, that just as a loaf is made up of many grains and a body is comprised of many members, so Christians together constitute the mystical Body of Christ. We confess this every time we celebrate the Lord's Supper. Not only do we thus identify ourselves with the Lord and rejoice in His saving work, but we announce that "we are one with every saint who loves His Name."

Here then is an important congregational aspect of the Supper; a tacit rejection of all that smacks of sectarianism and schismatic propaganda. Anthony Norris Groves (1795-1853), one of the early Christian Brethren, withdrew from the Church of England when he discovered that, as a lay missionary, he would not be allowed to celebrate the Lord's Supper unless a clergyman was present. Reprimanded by a friend, who was himself a minister in the Church, Groves wrote the following letter to him. We quote it here at some length since it so helpfully expresses important truth about true Christian communion.

> "You say I quitted your communion; if you mean by that, that I do not now break bread with the Church of England, this is not true, but if you mean that I do not exclusively join you, it is quite true, feeling this spirit of exclusiveness to be the very essence of schism which the apostle so strongly reproves in 1 Corinthians. I therefore know no distinction but am ready to break the bread and drink the cup of holy joy with all who love the Lord and will not lightly speak evil of His name. I feel every saint to be a holy person because Christ dwells in him and manifests Himself where he worships; and though his faults be as many as the hairs of his head, my duty still is, with my Lord, to join him as a member of the mystical body, and to hold communion and fellowship with him in any work of the Lord in which he may be engaged."[4]

---

4   F.R.Coad, *History of the Brethren Movement*, (Grand Rapids: Eerdmans. (1968). P.23.)

Any church, or group of churches, for that matter, that views itself as custodian of the Lord's Supper, with some imagined mandate to "guard the table" or say which Christians can or cannot enjoy communion, arrogates to itself an authority not countenanced by Scripture. How sad that something as inclusive as the Breaking of Bread should have been so misunderstood and misused as to be thought of as the exclusive privilege of a chosen few. Such thinking makes it man's table, not the Lord's!

The word *koinōnia* translated 'communion' in this context, means quite simply, 'fellowship'. It points to something which is held in common by all, or at least should be. What more beautiful word could be found to characterize the believer's privileges at the Lord's Supper? We might almost say that while Paul did not coin the word, when he applied it to the Christian celebration of remembrance, he gives it its richest connotation.

Remembrance

The words, *"Do this in remembrance of Me"* are found in the Lucan/Pauline record of the Last Supper (cf. 1Cor. 11:24-25; Luke 22:19). As already suggested, it is as though the Lord, anticipating our forgetfulness, makes specific provision for us. Paul notes Jesus' words, *"In remembrance of Me"* twice; once in relation to the bread and again in relation to the cup. For Him, this was evidently an important aspect of the Lord's Supper. He saw it as the living link between all true believers in Christ from His own time right through to the moment of the Saviour's return.

We note several points about this remembrance. First, it is an active remembrance, something we are expected to get involved in. Every time Christians break bread they do so together and in a deliberate act of remembrance. They do not meet together simply to reflect on historical events but gather around the same kind of emblems Jesus used when He instituted His Supper and do as He did. Whether they use leavened or unleavened bread; wine or grape juice is unimportant. What matters is that in the action or drama of the communion service there is a real commemoration. That is to say, involvement and action are essential parts of the event. There may be talking, singing, praying and meditating but the focus is the commemorative act.

There is something special about seeing the emblems. They are to faith, "the solemn sign of the heavenly and divine" to use the hymn writer's line. Obviously there is more to the Supper than bread and wine. However, these elements through faith and the gracious aid of the Holy Spirit, stimulate our worship. The emblems remain unchanged, having the substance as well as the "accidents" of bread and wine. They have no magical or supernatural qualities but are there as visual aids to remembrance.

Second, it is important to recognize that our remembrance is of a Person. Moreover, He is not simply a person who "was" but someone who "is". Usually, we remember things or people that have been part of history or part of our own past experience. The unique thing about the remembrance of Christ is that we are not only celebrating His historical Incarnation and saving work but our present relationship with Him as our Living Head and Great Priest. Yes, we recall the events of the Lord's life and His dreadful suffering, but that is only part of the story. We come together around His table to offer Him our thanks; to talk to Him, not simply about Him.

We submit that Christ is no more really present at a communion service than He is at a prayer meeting or family service. In fact, Jesus' promise, *"where two or three come together in My name, there am I with them"*, if read in context, relates to a prayer meeting, not some supposedly sacramental occasion. (cf. Matt. 18:20). How sad that such a wonderful text has sometimes been used as a kind of sectarian slogan!

The bread and wine, no matter how they are thought of, or however "consecrated" by a member of the clergy, offer no guarantee of Christ's presence. He is there because He delights to be with even the smallest possible quorum, *"two or three"*, of His assembled people. His presence is no less real because it is spiritual: it is certainly not imaginary. Since Jesus, our risen Lord, is no less a person than the God of the universe, not only is He capable of ubiquity but of omnipresence, by His Spirit. He needs no human assistance nor material emblem to give assurance of His presence. It surely bears repeating that when we come to the Table our focus should be on the Lord Himself, recognized as being present among us. As Jesus said, *"Do this for a remembrance of Me."*

William Cowper (1731-1800), expresses this so beautifully,

"Jesus where're Thy people meet,
There, they behold Thy mercy seat
Where're they seek Thee, Thou art found,
And every place is hallowed ground.

"For Thou, within no walls confined,
Inhabitests the humble mind;
Such ever bring Thee where they come,
And going, take Thee to their home."

Chapter 9

Covenant, Proclamation and Anticipation

Covenant

While all four institution narratives include references to the word 'covenant' (*diathēkē*), only Paul and Luke use the phrase *"the new covenant in My blood"* (Luke 22:20; 1 Cor. 11:25). This does not indicate two distinct strands or traditions of institution, as is sometimes suggested, but a confluence of various Old Testament covenant stories. Paul is offering both contrast and comparison, in order to sharpen his readers' appreciation of their privileges and responsibilities as guests at the Lord's Supper. While keeping in mind the various former covenants, the apostle focuses on two in particular. He wants his readers to reflect on the great Sinaitic Covenant—described by the author of Hebrews as *"the first covenant"* (Heb. 9:1). He reminds them that while their standing in Christ is reminiscent of Israel's covenant standing with Jehovah, they are even more secure. Whereas the "Old" or "First" Covenant was sealed by the blood of a sacrificial animal, the New Covenant is sealed by the blood of Christ. The contrast could hardly be greater!

It will be helpful to quote from the Exodus narrative here, in order to recognize the differences:

> *"Then he (Moses) took the Book of the Covenant and read it to the people. They responded "we will do every-thing the Lord has said; we will obey. Moses then took the blood, sprinkled it on the people and said, "This is*

the blood of the covenant that the Lord has made with
you in accordance with all these words:" (Ex. 24:7-8).

Now it is sometimes suggested that the Old Covenant, unlike the New, was a bilateral covenant which, while based on God's promise, depended on Israel's compliance. However, that argument cannot be sustained. After all, although we often think of the giving of the Law at Sinai as something harsh and foreboding, the truth is that the revelation and giving of the Law was an act of grace on God's part. In the Law with all its moral and ceremonial ramifications, God was not only revealing His will and showing man a road to blessing but providing a restraint on sin (cf. Rom. 3:20; 7:7-8; Gal. 3:23). This is not to say that the purpose of the Law was to save, clearly it was not. The Law was given to show man his sinfulness and cast him on his face before a Holy God. This is how Paul states it, *"What then was the purpose of the law? It was added because of the transgressions..."* (Gal. 3:19).

The apostle goes on to explain *"the law was our school master (paidagōgos) to bring us to Christ"* (*eis Christō* literally: 'unto Christ') (Gal. 3:25). God did not make His covenant at Sinai conditional upon Israel's agreement. He knew man was incapable of compliance with His will. Jehovah, acting in grace, gave His Law and established the Sinaitic Covenant quite independently of man. In that sense, it was unilateral, as the word *diathēkē* suggests. Israel's loud profession about keeping *"everything the Lord has said"* was, in the light of their subsequent performance, simply a vain promise but this did not negate the covenant. Obviously, disobedience robbed Israel of potential blessing but that was their problem not God's! In the divine scheme of things, it not only demonstrated the need for something better, but also anticipated the provision of such (cf. Heb. 10:9).

The contrast between the Old and the New Covenants is seen in at least two other areas. First and foremost, the new covenant is ratified by the precious blood of Christ. In his great covenant chapter, the writer of Hebrews tells us that, *"the blood of bulls and goats could never take away sin"* (Heb. 10:4,11). By contrast, sin is not only atoned for or covered, but put away by the Saviour's sacrifice. Second, the New Covenant does not demand blind conformity to rules and regulations but calls for a life of loving and glad obedience.

W. E. Vine writes: "In contradistinction to the English word 'covenant' (lit. 'a coming together') which signifies a mutual understanding between two parties or more, each binding himself to fulfill obligations, it (*diathēkē*) does not in itself contain the idea of joint obligation, it mostly signifies an obligation undertaken by a single person."[5]

Paul draws a comparison between our Lord's words of institution and the words of Jeremiah's ancient prophecy, which reads: *"'The time is coming', declares the Lord, when I will make a new covenant with the house of Israel and with the house of Judah. It will not be like the covenant I made with their forefathers… This is the covenant I will make… I will put My laws in their minds and write it on their hearts. I will be their God… For I will forgive their wickedness and will remember their sins no more".* (Jer. 31:31-34; cf. Heb.10). While Jesus and Jeremiah both refer to a "new covenant," (one which would be inward rather than outward, *"in hearts rather than in stone"*) Jeremiah's promise relates to something future. Jesus' words of institution point to a present experience. The New Covenant provisions of forgiveness and relationship with God are actually realized by virtue of the saving work of the Lord Jesus at Calvary.

There is more here. In His words *"the new covenant in My blood"*, Jesus is reminding His followers that they not only stand in a unique relationship to Himself, and are the recipients of His unmerited favour, but, that they also have a special commitment to Him. This means that in "the keeping of the feast" they and we, make tacit declaration of our acceptance of the responsibilities of our covenant relationship with Him.

The bread and the cup thus become covenant tokens; symbols of our pledge of loyalty to the Lord Jesus. We declare our willingness to live in accordance with the New Covenant. Thus we not only proclaim our status as beneficiaries but as covenant partners with Christ: those who will keep faith with Him.

---

5   W.E. Vine, *Expository Dictionary of New Testament Words,Vol.1*, p. 25

Proclamation

"For whenever you eat this bread and drink this cup you proclaim the Lord's death" (1 Cor. 11:26). In this distinctive Pauline view of the Lord's Supper, he reminds his readers that every time they participate in the Breaking of Bread they 'proclaim' or 'announce' (*katangellete*) the Lord's death. For the apostle, the Lord's Supper is a 'visible word.' To recall Augustine's phrase, a proclamation of the Good News of salvation. To use contemporary idiom, it is an audio-visual presentation of the story of our redemption.

Of course, Paul may also be making the point that the celebration of the Lord's Supper, should be accompanied by an oral proclamation of the Gospel. Significantly, his verb, *katangellō* means 'to tell fully'. It is used regularly in the New Testament for the public declaration of the Gospel (Acts 17:3, Acts 16:17; Rom. 1:8; 1 Cor. 9:14 Col. 1:28).

The apostle may well have in mind the fact that when the Jews celebrated their Passover meal, the haggadah (a lengthy narration of the Exodus story) was always an essential part of the proceedings. In any case, Paul is not so concerned with how we celebrate the Lord's Supper but with why we do it.

Surprisingly, it is a rare thing to find a church that deliberately celebrates the Lord's Supper as a means of evangelism. Indeed, sometimes in our zeal to "guard the table," we tend to exclude non-Christians even from observing. What more eloquent sermon than the declaration of the Person and work of Christ at the Lord's Supper? As another communion hymn puts it,

> "No Gospel like this feast
> Spread for thy Church by Thee;
> Nor prophets, nor evangelists
> Preach the glad news more free.
> All our redemption cost,
> All our redemption won;
> All it had won for us, the lost,
> All it cost Thee, the Son."

Elisabeth R. Charles.

However we may react to this suggestion today, it is obvious that whenever the early Christians came together to worship and celebrate the Lord's Supper, they expected unbelievers to be present. When speaking of such occasions, which evidently were quite unstructured, Paul makes a point of appealing for decorum and intelligibility — particularly for the sake of the visitors who would be there as observers and enquirers (cf. 1 Cor. 14:23-40).

Anticipation

Although there are distinctly eschatological references in the Synoptic narratives of the Last Supper, we owe the phrase, *"until He comes"* to Paul. In the Gospels Jesus talks about His drinking *"from the fruit of the vine anew in the kingdom of God"* (cf. Mark 14:25 cf. Matt. 26:29). Paul, on the other hand, relates the Lord's Supper not so much to the kingdom but to the coming of the King. This of course is what we might expect since he had not, as far as we know, seen Christ in the time of His incarnation.

This important eschatological emphasis is a reminder that every time Christians break bread they not only remember the Saviour's passion but anticipate His *parousia*!. For them, it is always, so to speak, "once more and once less!" The Lord's Supper is not only the link between the Advents but a dramatic statement that Jesus is at once, our risen and returning Lord. This anticipatory aspect of the Lord's Supper is of course both heartening and salutary. It not only encourages Christians to count on the living Christ being with them every day, but alerts them to live holy lives as they await His Coming. (cf. 1 John. 2:28 - 3:3). We look at the bread and cup on the table and realize that these 'signs to faith' will soon give place to sight.

Part 3

Contemporary Applications

"The offering of Christ once made is that perfect redemption, propitiation and satisfaction, for all the sins of the whole world, both original and actual; and there is none other satisfaction, but that alone. Wherefore the sacrifice of the Masses, in which it was commonly said, that the Priest did offer Christ for the quick and the dead, to have remission of pain or guilt, were blasphemous fables and dangerous deceits."

Article xxxi of the Articles of Religion (Also known as, *The 39 Articles*)
  —*Book of Common Prayer*

Chapter 10

New Testament Guidelines

"What Saith The Scripture?"

In order to find some practical guidelines for a communion service, it will be helpful to look for any scriptural precedents. This, however, will not be easy for various reasons. First, there is no definitive statement in the New Testament telling us how to conduct the "breaking of bread." There are one or two brief descriptions of the sort of thing that went on in those first church gatherings but nothing precise. Secondly, there is no consensus among Christians as to how we respond to biblical narrative. This is true even among Evangelicals who have a high view of Scripture. For example, some will argue that since it is impossible to recapture the historical and local milieu of primitive Christianity, it is impractical to attempt to replicate its methodology. This view is not necessarily born of theological perversity but from a desire to be open to discovering new, authentic forms of worship, under the Holy Spirit's direction and in keeping with scriptural principles.

Other Christians are equally convinced that the opposite is true. For them, the way things were done in the churches of New Testament times should be considered normative. It is not just a way of doing things but the way of doing things. They regard whatever order and forms of worship that may be found in the New Testament as patterns and precedents for worship in any age or situation. Keeping these disparate opinions in mind, let us take a look at the practices of the Primitive Church in relation to the Lord's Supper.

Celebration

While some may object to the use of the term celebration in describing participation in the Lord's Supper, it has a lot to commend it especially if we keep in mind the words, *"let us keep the festival"* - one dictionary definition of 'celebration' is, 'to publish abroad'. Whenever the early Christians met to break bread in remembrance of Christ, different thoughts and emotions must have surfaced, as indeed they do for ourselves. There would always have been a spirit of reverence, since the One they were remembering was non other than, the divine Lord of the universe. There would also have been feelings of sadness, as they reflected on the sufferings of Christ, which, by the way, some of them had personally witnessed. They could never forget the spiritual anguish as well as the dreadful, physical pain the Saviour endured, as He was cruelly put to death on the cross. Few deaths were more excruciating than crucifixion. On the other hand, there would have been a special spirit of praise and thanksgiving, leading to spontaneous expressions of joyful worship (cf. 1 Corinthians 14:26). Significantly, when describing the earliest occasions for Christian communion, Luke writes: *"They broke bread in their homes and ate together with glad and sincere hearts, praising God..."* (Acts 2:46-47). Evidently, celebration, was not a bad word as far as the early believers were concerned. Indeed, it may well sum up what is likely to happen still when Christians share in a communion gathering.

The manner in which we *"keep the festival"* will depend largely on our particular, ecclesiastical tradition. Some will meet formally, in the majestic surroundings of a beautiful cathedral, bathed in the warm light shining through stained glass windows and wrapped in the sounds of a mighty organ. Others will gather together in the contrived plainness of a silent meeting room. The one setting will make for solemnity and mystery; the other for quiet meditation and the contemplation of Scripture. Some congregations will celebrate communion weekly; some monthly; and some quarterly. Each will offer its own reason to be for doing it this way or that.

Informality

We discovered from our earlier consideration of the institution narratives that the Lord's Supper developed somewhat informally. Jesus and His disciples had been observing the Jewish Passover Seder. As they celebrated that ancient, religious, family meal, the Lord took some of the items that were on the table and used them to institute His own Supper. Typical of a Passover meal, the atmosphere would have been informal as everyone present would adopt the usual, reclining stance.

While Jesus clearly intended that His followers continue the practice of remembering Him, by sharing a cup and bread, He did not prescribe any particular occasion, liturgy or order of service. It is noteworthy that by their on-going, regular celebration of the Lord's Supper, the disciples showed they understood Jesus' request. They evidently recognized that it was something to be enjoyed frequently, not annually, like the Passover.

This same informality appears to have characterized the gatherings described in Acts. We discover that the breaking of bread (note the use of the definite article) is established early, as a regular feature of the corporate worship of the Jerusalem congregation (Acts 2:42). Indeed, it is sometimes difficult to know whether Luke is describing a social or a 'church meeting' (cf. v. 46). Reading between the lines, it appears that the first Christians met in groups, in different homes where they broke bread daily. Such home settings would naturally make for informality.

We can learn lessons from these early Christians. First, we need to resist thinking that this or that format for communion is the only authentic one. We may be sure that a certain orderliness characterized the basic biblical model, however, there appears to have been great flexibility. That surely is still the genius of the Lord's Supper: it can be enjoyed in many ways and in diverse situations, cultures and traditions.

Second, we should keep in mind the personal as well as the congregational aspects of the Lord's Supper. It is both a means of remembering our Lord and of expressing our oneness in Christ. It is unfortunate that something which is intended to unite Christians has often been so misinterpreted that it has divided them.

Third, in the light of its institution and practice in New Testament times, we would do well occasionally, to celebrate the Lord's Supper in the context of a church meal, rather than always in a more formal church setting. No doubt it would take a little getting used to, but it would be surprisingly stimulating in terms of real fellowship. It would also recapture the atmosphere of the early days of Christianity, when the Lord's Supper was associated with the *Agapē* or "Love feast." (cf. 2 Pet.2:13; Jude v.12; 1 Cor.11:20-22).

While other lessons can be learned and applied, two are important. On the one hand we need to differentiate between our own particular ecclesiastical traditions and early church customs. On the other hand, it is essential to keep before us the real purpose of the Lord's Supper. Of course, novelty hunting has no more to commend it than ecclesiastical tradition or habit. The important thing to keep in mind is that simple yet profound word of our Saviour, *"do this in remembrance of Me"*.

Frequency

Although we are given little information regarding the frequency of Early Church gatherings to break bread, one thing is clear, they met often. At first they broke bread daily, perhaps more by necessity than design, since communion, in those days as noted, was part of a communal meal. Following the Day of Pentecost, the Jerusalem Church had grown rapidly. As a result, the developing tension between official Jewry and the Christian community made it difficult for the Christians socially. They were ostracized and persecuted and many lost their means of livelihood. This meant that many of the believers were poor and very dependent on each other's hospitality and friendship.

When they met to share communal meals it seems they generally concluded the meal with a time of remembrance and breaking of bread. One can imagine that on those occasions various people present would offer personal testimonies and reminiscences of Jesus. As far as we can tell, it seems these daily gatherings gave way to weekly celebrations of the Lord's Supper. After the Resurrection of Christ, the Christians met together on the first day of the week, the Lord's Day, rather than on the Sabbath (John 20:19; Acts 20:7; 1 Cor. 16:2; Rev. 1:10). This was not only in recognition of the centrality of the Resurrection but a clear, statement of Christianity's break with Judaism.

There is an interesting story in Acts 20 concerning Paul's one week stay in Troas, on the return of his third missionary journey. We read: *"And upon the first day of the week when the disciples came together to break bread, Paul preached unto them."* (Acts 20:7 KJV).

Several things are worth noting here. First, it seems that it had already become customary for the Christians to meet together on the first day of the week, in order to break bread. Second, we note that they met in a commodious upstairs room, probably in someone's home. Third, the breaking of bread followed a lengthy discourse by Paul. As it happened, the celebration of the Lord's Supper was further delayed on this occasion, due to Eutychus' accident and recovery. Here is Luke's description of what happened, *"Paul went down, threw himself on the young man and put his arms around him. 'Don't be alarmed', he said. 'He's alive!' Then he went upstairs again and broke bread* (literally: "the loaf") *and ate"* (Acts 20:10-11).

Of course it could be argued that what is in view here is not a church gathering for the Breaking of Bread but rather an informal social gathering. However, a careful reading suggests that something more significant is in view. Luke's introductory words (and after all, he was an eyewitness) suggest that the main purpose of this Sunday gathering in Troas was *"to break bread"* (v. 7). It is unlikely he would not have written that had he merely been referring to a social meal: an almost daily occurrence in the early churches.

Judging from Luke's words in verse 11, what happened was that after Paul's sermon, which went on until midnight, proceedings were interrupted due to Eutychus' fatal fall. Then later, upon the young man's miraculous recovery, the group formally *"remembered the Lord,"* enjoyed a regular meal, then listened to Paul as he continued his talk until daybreak! One wonders how most modern western congregations would react to such an agenda, even if they knew it was the preacher's last visit!

Prof. F. F. Bruce has an interesting comment and a footnote regarding this historic occasion. He writes, "It was probably past midnight (and therefore properly Monday morning) when they broke the bread and took their fellowship meal."[6]

His footnote reads, "In v.11 *klasas ton arton* (where the article points back to *klasai arton* in v.7) refers to the eucharistic breaking of the bread, while *geusamenos* refers to the fellowship meal."[7]

The only other evidence we have for these congregational gatherings is to break bread (1 Cor. 11:18ff). There Paul writes, *"In the first place, I hear that when you come together as a church, there are divisions among you, and to some extent I believe it. When you come together, it is not the Lord's Supper you eat, for as you eat, each of you goes ahead without waiting for anybody else. One remains hungry, another gets drunk."* (1 Cor. 11:18-21). Granted, Paul is speaking ironically here, exposing the unacceptable behaviour of some of the Christians at Corinth. Nevertheless, his words indicate that there were recognized, regular, congregational gatherings to break bread.

While offering no description of proceedings, if we read the apostle's words in the general context of 1 Corinthians chapters 11-14, he is probably thinking of the Breaking of Bread as part of an unstructured gathering, at which people were free to exercise their spiritual gifts, in an orderly manner (see 1 Corinthians 14:26 and 40). Clearly, there was nothing prescribed nor any ritualistic rite.

Two other references underline the Early Church's commitment to celebrating the Lord's Supper regularly. The first is Paul's double use of the adverb *hosakis* ("whenever" or "as often as") in 1 Corinthians 11:25 and 26 (used elsewhere in the New Testament only once in Rev. 11:6). He does not specify how often they broke bread but his words suggest they did it frequently.

---

6   F.F. Bruce, NICNT, The Book of Acts, (Grand Rapids: Eerdmans,), p. 409.

7   cf. footnote # 26

The second is Hebrews 10:25, where speaking of the importance of personal holiness, worship and the *parousia*, (ideas all associated with the Lord's Supper) the writer urges regularity upon his readers. There can be little doubt that in the early churches, the breaking of bread played a very important and integral part of worship. If we are looking for patterns for our worship, the New Testament supports the idea that we break bread regularly and frequently.

Celebrant

There is not the slightest suggestion in the New Testament that the celebration of the Lord's Supper, required the services of an apostle, or of some other specially qualified individual. Indeed, that would seem to run counter to the clear emphasis laid on the doctrine of the priesthood of all believers and would have been unlikely (1 Pet. 2:5,9; 1 Tim. 2:5-6).

Although the apostles and subsequently the elders, were accepted as leaders in the New Testament churches, they were never cast in a priestly role or viewed as having any special sacerdotal privileges not enjoyed by other Christians. There might or might not be an elder present to break the bread. In the Early Churches, it evidently did not matter. It is singularly unfortunate that with the development of ecclesiastical hierarchies and the installation of "ordained clergy," we have, by and large, lost this scriptural emphasis on "body-life" and universal priesthood.

Many modern churches, even good evangelical ones, require the presence of a member of the clergy, before they can convene a communion service. Now, while Paul always insisted on good taste and due order, he might well have been amused at some of our rules and regulations about the Lord's Supper (cf. 1 Cor. 14:40).

The only qualifications for ministry Paul and his contemporaries recognized were, spiritual gift, purity of life and congregational recognition. Howard Marshall writes, "The New Testament says nothing about who should conduct or celebrate the sacrament, and there is no evidence whatever that anything corresponding to our modern 'ordination' was essential. The celebration of the sacrament today should not be confined to those ordained to the ministry by the laying on of hands but should be open to any believer authorized by the church to do so."[8]

Elsewhere he comments, "Paul says nothing about which members of the church were entitled to lead in the celebration; it was evidently not a matter of any concern to him. We may assume that it would be one of the people who devoted themselves to the service of the saints; to use Paul's own rather vague terms for church workers (1 Cor. 16:15); in any case, there seems to have been no dissension on those points."[9]

Whenever the early Christians assembled to break bread or, for that matter, to do anything else relating to the assembly, they all met on an equal footing. None dictated to the other and no one presumed to act in a perfunctory, priestly fashion, as if to mediate for the rest. The only New Testament grounds for disqualification were, deliberate and unjudged sins, such as sexual perversion, immorality, drunkenness, idolatry, swindling, slandering, causing division (1 Cor. 5:10-13; 6:9-11; Rom. 16:17; Titus 3:10).

Participation

The New Testament seems to make it plain that just as all who believed were baptized, so all who believed were free and indeed, expected to share in the Lord's Supper. There were no qualifying ceremonies or prerequisites, such as baptism, confirmation or church membership. Since it was the Lord's Table, it was open to all the Lord's people. This may sound strange to those sectarian types and groups who have arbitrarily established their own criteria for deciding who is welcome to break bread with them. In fact, one sometimes gets the uncomfortable feeling that such people are more anxious to exclude, than include other believers.

8   ibid., Marshall p.156
9   ibid., p. 112

Something else, quite foreign to the New Testament, is the suggestion that when Christians assemble to take communion, only the priest-celebrant should be allowed to drink from the cup. Our Lord's words are unequivocal in this regard. When He instituted His Supper He said concerning the cup: *"Drink from it all of you"* (Matt. 26:27; 1 Cor. 11:25). That the disciples understood Him is equally clear. Mark writes: *"Then He took the cup, gave thanks and offered it to them, and they all drank from it"* (Mark 14:23).

Preparation

Worship is a two-way experience. Primarily, it is an expression of our heart-felt devotion to God; born of an appreciation of His Son, our Lord and Saviour, Jesus Christ. Yet there is always another side, the spiritual renewal graciously effected by the Holy Spirit in our hearts as worshippers. This is certainly the case when we come together to break bread. Having said that, worship is at its best when offered from a prepared heart. As in so many areas of life, "you get out of it what you put into it!" This should not be construed as a mechanical view of worship but rather as a plea for preparedness as we come to the Lord's Table. Even in those celebrations of communion where "everything is done up front" with no opportunity given for audible "lay involvement", preparation is still rewarding. In Old Testament times, when people approached the Lord in worship, they are said to have come with *"full baskets"* (Ex. 29:3; Deut. 26:2-4). Indeed it was a prerequisite - *"none shall appear (before the Lord) empty"* (Ex. 23:15; 34:30).

We have already observed the absence of a prescribed order for communion in the New Testament. Similarly, aside from Paul's exhortation to prior self-examination, nothing is said about how to prepare for the Lord's Supper. However, in the light of biblical teaching about worship, it is obvious that some things are essential. First and foremost, we must come as cleansed worshippers. We must take time to make sure that we are right with the Lord and with our fellow Christians. We should also seek to cultivate a close relationship with the

Saviour, through prayer, personal communion and meditation on the scriptures. If we come to communion hurriedly, carelessly or late, we should not be surprised if things seem dull, lifeless or boring. Relationships take time to cultivate. Communion is really fellowship with the Lord and His people and any worthwhile fellowship involves thoughtfulness and understanding.

Chapter 11

Enjoying Christ's Presence

While little can be added to the great body of eucharistic doctrine developed by the Church over the centuries, it is important for today's Christians to consider the great question: How is Christ's Presence realized at His Supper? While Scripture remains constant and peerless in its authority, as the Living Word of God, it continually challenges us to make practical application of its truth in each generation. Bearing this in mind, in this chapter we shall re-examine some aspects of eucharistic theology in light of today's needs.

How Is Christ Present?

Few questions have generated more discussion and dissent across the centuries of Church history, than this one: "How is Christ present in the Breaking of Bread?" Some have opted for the "real presence" of the Saviour. They believe that the bread and wine are changed into His flesh and blood. Others teach that Christ's physical, "local presence" is actually realized but, "alongside the bread and wine". Others insist that Christ is present spiritually, not physically, but sacramentally. Commemorationists believe that Christ's presence at His Supper, is made known to His people, through the gracious ministry of the Holy Spirit, just as it is on any other occasion when they meet in His Name. We shall of course meet these interpretations later when we consider something of the history of the doctrine of the Lord's Supper.

What are we to make of these various opinions? Can we respond to true believers who hold these various views today and say something which is both biblically based and conciliatory in tone? Perhaps a starting place is to stress the great promise made by our Lord Himself, *"for where two or three come together in my name, there am I with them"* (Matt.18:20). Granted, these words are not spoken in a eucharistic setting but in the context of teaching about Church life, inter-personal relationships and prayer.

What is Jesus saying? He is promising that, whereas according to Jewish tradition a ten man quorum is required to establish a Synagogue congregation, the smallest possible quorum. *"two or three,"* meeting together, in Christ's name, has the guarantee of His presence with them. The only criteria are: recognition of His authority (i.e. "in My Name") and the acceptance of each other (note the word "together.")

If then we are asked, in the light of Scripture, to say how Christ is "present" at a communion service, we would respond that in accordance with His own promise; He is present always when His followers meet in His Name. Of course, that answer will not satisfy the sacerdotalist nor the sacramentalist but hopefully it might help to bring separated brethren together. After all, true believers will surely be more concerned to experience and enjoy the presence of Christ than to explain the "mechanics", so to speak.

If we are pressed further to say exactly how this presence of Christ is realized by believers, we would say, "by the ministry of the Holy Spirit." We have Jesus' own words of confirmation on this. Speaking of the Spirit, His 'alter ego'; Jesus said, *"I will not leave you as orphans; I will come to you"* (John 15:18). Then, as He goes on to describe the work of the Holy Spirit in relation to Himself, He says, *"He will bring glory to Me by taking from what is Mine and making it known to You. All that belongs to the Father is Mine. That is why I said the Spirit will take from what is Mine and make it known to You"* (John 16:14-15). Boethia Thompson's communion hymn expresses this truth beautifully:

> "Jesus, Lord , we know Thee present
> At Thy table freshly spread
> Seated at Thy priceless banquet,
> With Thy banner overhead,

"Precious moments at Thy table,
From all fear and doubt set free;
Here to rest, so sweetly able,
Occupied alone with Thee.

"Here rejoicing in Thy nearness,
Gladly by Thy Spirit led;
Calmly in the blest remembrance
Of Thy precious blood once shed.

"Lord, we take each simple token
In fond memory of Thee;
Muse upon Thy body broken,
And Thy blood shed on the tree."

The Communion Of The Body Of Christ

Whatever our view of the Church, one truth held in common by most Christians is that we are one with every saint who loves His name. This idea of unity, perhaps "union" is a better word, between Christians is both symbolically and actually realized in the Breaking of Bread. We go back again to Paul's question, *"Is not the cup of thanksgiving for which we give thanks a participation (koinōnia) in the blood of Christ? And is not the bread that we break a participation in the body of Christ?"* (1 Cor.10:16). He then goes on to explain, *"Because there is one loaf, we, who are many, are one body, for we all partake of the one loaf"*. The apostle is underlining two truths here. First, that our actual participation in the cup and the loaf symbolizes our common sharing in Christ.

As Zwingli wrote: "Those that eat and drink at this (table) become one body and one bread; that is, all who assemble here for the purpose of proclaiming the Lord's death and eating the symbolic bread, certainly show that they are the Body of Christ, that is members of His Church, which as it has one faith and eats the symbolical bread, so is one body and one bread. Thus it becomes clear that Christ wishes to give us bread and wine as food and drink, because as they two are combined each into one body from numberless grains and atoms of flour or grapes of the vine, so we come together into one faith and one body."[10]

In 1 Cor. 10, Paul (who obviously believed in communion in both kinds) is saying in effect, that as each believer takes his morsel of the loaf or his sip from the cup, he is declaring his union with Christ in His incarnation and sacrifice. He is as well, attesting his mystical union with all his brothers and sisters in Christ. As we saw earlier, this truth was not appreciated in the church at Corinth, hence Paul's serious words about divine judgement on their failure *"to discern the Lord's body,"* (1 Cor. 11:29). Beside this symbolical statement, there is also the actualizing of our communion in the physical eating and drinking together that is central in any Breaking of Bread meeting.

We have seen earlier that sharing food and drink, a basic human experience, has sacred ramifications in some cultures. To eat a man's food or accept his hospitality is a tacit acceptance of his friendship: a kind of mutual pledge not to harm him or be harmed by him (cf. John 13:18 and Ps. 41:9).

We certainly need to restate this aspect of the Lord's Supper today. Faced with our contemporary proliferation of denominations and confessions, we need to be reminded that true Christian unity is important, even essential to our effective witness in the world (cf. John 17:11,21).

Experiencing Forgiveness

Clearly, while participation in the Lord's Supper is no automatic guarantee of the forgiveness of sins nor the communication of grace, there is certainly good news for sinners there! As we come to the Supper many things come to mind, not least that we are there as undeserving guests; sinners who depend on the amazing grace of God. However, hardly are we made aware of our sin, than God's gracious Holy Spirit reminds us of our Saviour's words, *"This is my blood of the covenant, which is poured out for many, for the forgiveness of sins"* (Matt. 26:28).

---

10   Corpus Reformatorum, Vol .3, Ed. Engli and Finster, (Leipzig). . pp.802-3.

As we take the bread and share in the cup we are comforted in remembering that, *"the blood of Jesus Christ, His Son cleanses us from all sin"* (cf. 1 John 1:9). We reject those Satanic insinuations and lies about our worthlessness and sin, and rejoice in the Lord's complete forgiveness. As someone has put it, "Satan loves to makes us bleed for wounds that are already healed!" Let us listen again to the Saviour's words, *"My body given for you... My blood poured out for you"*.

As we sit at the table, the reality of Christ's atonement is clearly brought to our notice. The Lord's Supper reminds us of that great hour at Calvary when, *"For He hath made Him to be sin for us, who knew no sin, that we might be made the righteousness of God in Him"* (2 Cor. 5:21). It tells us too, that the great stone was rolled away when Jesus rose as Conqueror of death and all our foes. Such are the solid grounds of Christian faith displayed at the table. Beside the objective, visual elements, there is the subjective side of communion and of our acceptance by God. The Holy Spirit makes real to our faith, the assurance of God's forgiveness. The invisible is made visible; the intangible palpable and our confidence is renewed.

Practicing Priesthood

For too long the so-called 'Mystery of the Eucharist' has been the guarded province of professional clergy. As a result, all kinds of strange ideas and superstitious practices have developed which in turn, have occasioned fear, misunderstanding and division. It is time to restate the great Reformation doctrine of the priesthood of all believers particularly as it relates to the Lord's Supper. After all, everything about the feast is completely open, immediate and available to all the people of God.

Scripture nowhere suggests for example, that the consecration and administration of the Lord's Supper are in any sense, sacerdotal acts. Neither the Lord Jesus nor His apostles state explicitly or implicitly, that only a specially qualified person can function as celebrant at Communion. Of course, some people will feel more comfortable observing and having things done for them "up front" at the Supper. However, such an attitude may well be a mark of spiritual laziness or worse, theological ignorance. Certainly order, decorum and reverence are important, but that does not mean that prescribed liturgies or qualified celebrants are necessary.

When Christians meet to worship at the Lord's Table, while rejecting any thought of a literal sacrifice of Christ, they are nevertheless privileged to offer spiritual sacrifices. These will include the consecration of themselves (Rom. 12:1 cf. 2 Tim. 4:6 and Ps. 51:17); the offering of thanksgiving, prayer and praise (Ps. 50:14; 107:22; 141:2; Hos. 14:2 and Heb. 13:15); and the giving of their material means in support of the Lord's work and on behalf of the needy (Heb. 13:16; Phil. 4:15-18).

Despite an absence of prescribed patterns of worship, the New Testament sees at least two things happening on the first day of the week, namely, the breaking of bread and the collection (Acts 20:7; 1 Cor. 16:1-2). Other priestly functions that may well be stimulated by a thoughtful participation in communion are the exercise of natural talents and spiritual gifts; the proclamation of the Gospel, the dispensing of hospitality and missionary service (cf. 2 Cor. 8:7-9; Rom. 15:16; 1 Pet. 4:9-11).

It is not surprising that when Christians are spiritually renewed and reading their Bibles, they tend to enjoy an informal, inclusive, unstructured style of Breaking of Bread. It is noteworthy that in those parts of the world where Christians live under totalitarian regimes and are denied their religious freedom, their simple gatherings to remember the Saviour become their very spiritual life blood. The fact that some of their leaders are unable to be present, because they have been imprisoned for the Gospel, in no way impedes nor precludes their celebration of the Lord's Supper.

Hopefully a careful study of New Testament ecclesiology will not only generate a renewed sense of our universal, royal and holy priesthood, but lead to a deeper appreciation of Him who, as both our Sacrifice and Priest, invites each of us to come to His Supper to remember Him.

Living Victoriously

The Lord's Supper is also a challenge to holy living, reminding us to have done away with the "leaven of malice and wickedness." How can we remember the Saviour of sinners and continue to live in sin? That surely would be the worst form of hypocrisy.

This gives rise to a further question, "who should be allowed to participate in the Lord's Supper and who should be excluded?" The answer is not easy because none of us feels worthy to be guests there. Most Christians would agree that there is something special about a communion service. It is a most significant occasion that calls for due preparation and self-examination. As Paul advises: *"a man ought to examine himself before he eats of the bread and drinks of the cup"* (1 Cor. 11:28).

Surely, the basic requirement for participation in the Lord's Supper is saving faith in Christ. How can an unbeliever enjoy any sense of a vital communion with the Saviour, with whom he has no personal relationship? It is not enough simply to give verbal assent to a Christian Creed, or to produce a baptismal certificate. There should be a credible confession of personal faith in Jesus Christ as Lord. But, there is more, Christians may disqualify themselves from participation at the Lord's Supper, through deliberate and unconfessed sin. It is evident from the apostle's severe words to the Corinthians, that their conduct not only disqualified them, but made a mockery of both the Church and the Lord's Supper.

As we come to break bread we are called to separation from sin and commitment to holy living. The very emblems before us remind us not only of the tremendous price paid for our redemption but of our spiritual union with Christ, in His death, burial and resurrection. Paul's question to his readers is, *"How shall we, that are dead to sin, live any longer therein?"* (Rom. 6:2).

After all, it is not the physical eating of the bread, nor the drinking of the wine that makes a person holy, but, to use Peter's phrase, it is *"the answer of a good conscience toward God"* that matters (cf. 1 Pet. 3:3). There is truth in the saying, "while sin may keep us from the Lord's Supper, the Lord's Supper may well keep us from sin." That is not to suggest a kind of magically communicated perfectionism but rather, a spiritual apprehensiveness about sin, born of our expectation of meeting Christ at His Table.

A further caution may be helpful. While spiritual self examination is important, we need to beware of an exaggerated sense of unworthiness that may cause us to absent ourselves from the Lord's Supper. None of us is worthy to be there. We come as, *"sinners saved by grace."* As the apostle puts it, *"Let a man examine himself and so let him eat…"* (1 Cor. 11:28).

The story is told of a famous Scottish pastor who observed a communicant tearfully declining the bread and the cup. Understanding something of the person's problems, the pastor whispered in her ear, "Take it woman, it is for sinners". Thank God, it is!

The Renewal Of Mission

If there is ever a place where a Christian is given fresh vision and impetus for his or her mission, it is at the Table of the Lord. Here, dramatically portrayed, is the heart of the Christian Gospel: *"Jesus Christ and Him crucified"* (1 Cor. 2:1). The emblems, simple though they may be, are eloquent in terms of Christian truth. The bread reminds us that He who became flesh for us sinners and our salvation, lives forever as a glorified Man in Heaven. He who for a little while was *"lower than the angels in order that He might die for us, is now crowned with glory and honour"* (Heb. 2:9).

The cup assures us that there is pardon *"for sins of deepest dye"*. It tells us that we can go forth with a message to the world that:

> "There is plentiful redemption
> In the blood that has been shed
> There is joy for all the members
> In the sorrows of the Head."

(F. W. Faber 1814-63)

No wonder Paul said *"We proclaim the Lord's death until He comes"*. Have our hearts grown cold or unconcerned? Is our congregation unduly proud of its million dollar sanctuary: impressed by its balanced budget: titillated by its latest charismatic experience, yet altogether lacking in evangelistic zeal and passion for lost souls? If so, then we need to come again contritely and humbly, to the Supper of the Lord, seeking to be renewed in our vision and mission.

Let the words of another communion hymn stir our resolve:

> "Power to feel thy love,
> And all its depths to know:
> Power to fix the heart above,
> And die to all below.

> "Power to keep the eye
> Forever fixed on Thee;
> Power to lift the warning cry
> To souls from wrath to flee.

> "Power lost souls to win
> From Satan's mighty hold;
> Power the wanderers to bring
> Back to the heavenly fold."

> (C. Russell Hurditch)

Renewal Of Hope

Whenever Christians sit down together to celebrate the Lord's Supper they are reminded of the promise of Jesus' personal Return. At the Last Supper, on the eve of His death, Our Lord Jesus told His disciples that the next time He would *"drink of the fruit of the vine"* would be, *"anew (with them) in my Father's Kingdom"* (Matt. 26:29). There, was a secure ground of hope: a promise, not only that Jesus would reign, but that His followers would reign with him. The celebration might be delayed, but its fulfillment will not be denied.

The Cross loomed before Him but the Glory and Crown lay ahead (cf. Heb. 12:2). Paul picks up this eschatological note and tells his readers that every time they break bread they proclaim the Lord's death *"until He comes"* (1 Cor. 11:26). The "blessed hope" which is such an essential feature of any true celebration of the Lord's Supper, is founded on both dominical promise and apostolic teaching. The Lord's Supper announces to men and angels that Jesus is coming again. In our technologically advanced but despairing, morally bankrupt society, the Lord's Supper proclaims hope. It reminds us that man does not have the last word, God does! The Church may look like an inconsequential anachronism to the media pundits, but when she spreads the table of her Lord, she looks forward to the day when she will be seen to be, *"Fair as the moon, clear as the sun and terrible as an army with banners"* (Song 6:10).

Chapter 12

Breaking Bread Together

In this chapter we shall look at a typical service for the Breaking of Bread as convened among a small group of churches known as, Christian Brethren. We are not suggesting that this is the only scriptural way of conducting such a service but it is an interesting attempt to replicate the way the Early Church might have celebrated the Lord's Supper. In point of fact, what we describe here may not be exactly what a visitor finds in every Brethren assembly since each is autonomous and likely to apply this general pattern in different ways. However, here is a style of celebrating the Supper which is quite versatile and free of ceremonial and denominational prerequisites.

Christian Brethren describe their weekly gathering for communion in various ways. For example, they may speak of it as, The Breaking of Bread, The Remembrance Meeting, The Lord's Supper, The Worship Meeting or simply as Communion. They do not use terms like, Holy Communion, The Eucharist or The Sacrament. In the congregation in England, where my own family worshipped, it was known as, The Morning Meeting. This reflects a distinct preference among Brethren to break bread in the morning of each Lord's Day.

Order Of Service

It will surprise a first-time visitor to discover that when Brethren meet to break bread there is no set order of service, nor anyone up front, in charge of the service. This reflects two things: first, their strong insistence on the priesthood of all believers, and second, their hope that there will be a reverent spontaneity in the worship, under the sensed superintendence of the Holy Spirit. Although this lack of structure may seem odd, even threatening to someone used to regular liturgies and directing clergy, it can sometimes be surprisingly fruitful in terms of worship.

Some assemblies (the name many Brethren prefer for their churches), are not adverse to a minimum of arrangement at the Lord's Supper. For example, one of the elders or a designated person, may give a brief introduction to the service. This may include, words of welcome, especially to any who are recognized as visitors; a brief explanation of the purpose and general procedure; and perhaps a hymn, prayer or Bible reading. However, for the most part, the meeting will be open for thoughtful, spontaneous participation, by the male members of the congregation.

As the service proceeds there will often be quite a lot of singing. Music has always played an important part in this kind of remembrance meeting and the Brethren have a great heritage of hymns for worship and communion which sadly, are not well-known outside their circle. Sometimes the singing is unaccompanied. Nowadays, in many places, there is an increasing use of praise songs.

There are likely to be several *ex tempore* prayers of thanksgiving, with quite moving expressions of appreciation of the Person and work of Christ. It is not unusual for such prayers to be addressed to the Risen Lord directly, who is recognized as being present by His Spirit, among His gathered people. Brethren make much of the text, *"where two or three are gathered together in My name, there am I in their midst of them"* (Matt. 18:20). This active recognition of the living presence of Christ is certainly a stimulus to the worship.

Short scripture readings, with or without comment, also play a part in the meeting. The emphasis will be on passages that encourage worship and praise. Sometimes a particular theme or focus becomes obvious and will be developed by those who take part. Teaching and exhortation regarding practical Christian living usually follow the actual sharing of the emblems. Indeed, in some assemblies there will be a set time for consecutive Bible teaching following the Breaking of Bread. This instruction may be presented by a teaching elder or by a visiting speaker, and may follow a pre-arranged syllabus of biblical study or doctrine.

The central feature of the service is the sharing of the bread and the cup. In some groups one person will give thanks for the bread and another for the cup; in others, the same individual does both. This person will then break the loaf apart and see that it is passed from hand to hand among the congregation. This procedure is repeated in connection with the cup. In larger congregations individuals are often appointed to facilitate these proceedings. In most assemblies a single loaf of bread is used. While some groups prefer a single communion cup, others, either because of local government health department by-laws, or by congregational preference, use individual cups. Following the sharing of the elements, an offering is taken, and in most assemblies this is the only offering taken weekly.

Interpretation

Generally speaking, the Brethren interpretation of the Lord's Supper approximates more closely to the so-called Zwinglian view. They do not usually regard the Supper as a Means of Grace, except in some secondary sense. Their emphasis will be on commemoration and communion, not on the communication of Grace. They regard the supper as a visual reminder of our Lord's Person and saving work but in no sense as a sacrifice.

If asked in what sense Christ is present at the Breaking of Bread, Brethren would probably affirm that He is present by His Holy Spirit. They would disavow all suggestions of the "local" or so-called, "real" presence of Christ (using those terms in their technical sense). However, despite this insistence, few people who have attended this kind of breaking of bread service would deny that often they have been acutely aware of the spiritual presence of the Lord.

One other emphasis should be noted here. While Brethren regard the Lord's Supper as a proclamation of the death, burial and resurrection of Jesus, they are very aware of its eschatological implications. It is doubtful whether a Breaking of Bread service passes without some reference being made to the Second Coming of the Lord Jesus. Of course, eschatology has always been a strong point of emphasis among Brethren. One wonders whether this is the result or reason for the central place the Lord's Supper is given in Brethren assemblies.

Brethren generally practice open communion, welcoming all professing believers in Christ to participate. They discourage non-Christians from taking communion, while welcoming any person to come and observe. Baptism, while not regarded a prerequisite for taking part in communion, is generally seen as a desirable, preparatory step. Unfortunately, there are some more conservative groups particularly in North America, even among so-called "Open Brethren," who belie their name and receive only those deemed to be from their circle of fellowship.

Despite their sometimes deserved image of being separatist and aloof, Brethren are, in principle at least, committed to the doctrine of the Oneness of all Christian believers. In fact this truth was a foundational principle in the early days of the Brethren movement, back in the eighteen thirties. To a large degree, it was this great scriptural truth that prompted their withdrawal from the established, denominational churches. Perhaps it is their zeal for orthodoxy, in terms of Christian doctrine, as well as their desire for purity of life, that leads some of their number to be quite strict in "guarding the table." Hopefully, a happy balance can be struck between "receiving all whom Christ has received and having *no fellowship with the unfruitful works of darkness*" (cf. Rom. 15:7; 2 Cor. 6:14). We shall be wise to adopt the attitude of Jesus rather than that of His zealous but misguided disciples (cf. Luke 9:49-50).

Chapter 13

Hymns for the Lord's Supper

Singing has always played an important part in Christian worship; never more so than at the Lord's Supper. Such expressions of worship are to be expected for obvious reasons, not least that at the conclusion of the Last Supper, Jesus joined His disciples in singing a hymn (cf. Matt. 26:30; Mark 14:26). We are not told what they sung but, more than likely, it was the last three Psalms from the "Egyptian Hallel" – (the name given to Psalms 113-118, regularly sung at Passover season).

This is how Paul describes an early Christian meeting of the church at Corinth, which would almost certainly have included the Breaking of Bread: " *When you come together everyone has a hymn (psalm), or a word of instruction, a revelation, a tongue or an interpretation. All these must be done for the strengthening of the church.*" (1 Cor. 14:26). His particular concern, was that the singing like every other activity in worship, be both intelligent and orderly, (cf. 1 Cor. 14:15,40). We should note that some expositors wonder if Paul's words here are not describing an acceptable pattern of worship but offering an exposé of the kind of confusion that characterized church gatherings at Corinth.

The New Testament has a number of references to music and poetry. For example, there are the great songs associated with the Nativity, Mary's Magnificat (Luke 1:46-55); the Angels' Gloria in excelsis (Luke 2:14) and Simeon's *nunc dimittis* (Luke 2:29-32). In Ephesians, Paul talks about *"psalms, hymns and spiritual songs"* and recommends that his readers *"sing and make melody in your heart (literally: 'with your heart') to the Lord"* (Eph. 5:19 cf. Col. 3:16). John the Seer introduces us to several anthems of praise, in the

Apocalypse (see Rev. 4:8, 11; 5:9-10, 12, 13; 7:12; 11:17-18; 15:3-4; 19:1-8). Beside these specific references to singing, there are several so-called, hymnic fragments found in the New Testament (including: Rom. 9:33-35; Eph. 4:14; Phil. 2:6-11; 1 Tim. 1:17; 6:15-16). It is usually understood that these snatches of poetry are from hymns used in the early Christian gatherings.

Quite apart from the regular hymns and music of the Church, a great body of musical liturgy has developed across the centuries, in connection with various, traditional celebrations of the Eucharist. For example, the Catholic Church, has long popularized its celebration of the Mass by means of music. The names of many of the great composers are all associated with their various "Masses" and "Requiems".

Further evidence of early musical requiem Masses can also be seen in many of the old church buildings in Europe. For example, in England, visitors will be shown a church's "Chantry". This small chapel is so named because in it the priest would sing Mass "on behalf of the souls of the departed"; particularly of course, the souls of the patrons who endowed the building and the benefice! However, although this might be an interesting area of study, it lies outside the scope and purpose of this book.

Here we shall simply take notice of some of the many lovely hymns that have been specially written for use at the Lord's Supper. Each of the main branches of the Protestant community has produced its hymns for communion. The eighteenth and nineteenth centuries saw a spate of such hymns. It was thought that this emphasis on hymn singing at the Lord's Supper was new but in fact, it was the recovery of a popular feature of early Church worship.

The most prolific hymn-writers of these later centuries were Isaac Watts and Charles Wesley (John Wesley to a lesser degree). Remarkably, Charles Wesley composed at least six thousand hymns! Among their hymns, these brothers produced a large number written for Communion. Isaac Watts, in his famous, *Hymns and Spiritual Songs*, published in 1707, devotes, the entire third section to, "Hymns Prepared for the Holy Ordinance of the Lord's Supper". This is a remarkable collection of forty-five hymns, unfortunately, many of them are little known or used today. The Wesley's story is similar. A collection of their hymns published in 1745, entitled "Hymns on the Lord's Supper," includes no less than one hundred and sixty-six such compositions. It is worth mentioning here, that the Wesleys and their friends at Oxford were not only called the Methodists but the Sacramentalists, a name reflecting their original practice of celebrating The Lord's Supper daily. The section headings of their collection of communion hymns, that follow, clearly demonstrates the eucharistic theology of John and Charles Wesley.

Part I.   As it is a memorial of the suffering
           and death of Christ
Part II.   As it is sign and Means of Grace
Part III. The Sacrament and Pledge of Heaven
Part IV.   The Holy Eucharist as it implies sacrifice
Part V.   Concerning the Sacrifice of our persons
Part VI.   After the Sacrament

Another large body of communion hymns, many written in the nineteenth century, originates with the Christian Brethren, the group of churches we looked at in the previous chapter. As we saw, Brethren place considerable stress on the importance of a regular, weekly gathering for the Breaking of Bread. Their emphasis on open worship, with special place being given to *ex tempore* prayers of thanksgiving and hymn singing, naturally gave birth to a large number of communion hymns, some of which have come into general use.

Three of the most prolific, Brethren hymn writers were: Robert C. Chapman (1803-1902) of Barnstaple, Devon; Sir Edward Denny (1796-1889) of Tralee Castle, Co. Kerry, Ireland; and J. George Deck (1807-1884), formerly of Somerset but later of New Zealand. Other hymn writers from among the Brethren include: John Nelson Darby (1800-1882); Samuel Prideaux Tregelles (1813-1875) the famous textual critic; Thomas Kelly

(1821-1906); J. Denham Smith (1817-1889); Frances Bevan (1827-1909); S.Trevor Francis (1834-1925); Lucy Bennett (1850-1927); Ada Habersham (1861-1918) and George Goodman (1866-1944). It is unfortunate that this rich collection of hymns for worship at the Lord's Supper is not better known and more widely used.

Admittedly, hymnology is not theology and obviously we need to be careful to keep our creedal priorities straight. However, having said that, we believe there is great benefit to be derived from the many moving expressions of worship and spiritual truth provided for us by Christian hymnists. On a personal note, I am particularly grateful to have been reared in the setting of an English village chapel, where, despite a comparative neglect of the great body of Christian oratorios and the like, strong emphasis was placed on the careful use and appreciation of communion hymns. Surprisingly, in such an unsophisticated environment, musically speaking, people were as discriminating about the tunes as the hymns they sang, especially at the Lord's Supper. I recall listening, as a child, to discussions about "suitable tunes" and even metrical details. It was not unusual to hear someone announce a hymn at the Breaking of Bread meriting with the added request that it be sung to a certain tune which they would then name! Of course we sang the hymns a cappella. That may sound quite passé today, especially in light of some of the modern worship songs.

Who is to deny then that the great value and purpose of hymns is to furnish the ordinary Christian with a means of expressing his or her intelligent worship? This is specially true of communion hymns. After all, the Lord's Supper should be regarded as an experience enjoyed and participated in, by all God's people. The great body of communion hymns can help us in this regard.

Here is an extract from the Preface to John Wesley's "A Collection of Hymns for the use of people called Methodists", written in London on October 24th, 1779:

> "I would recommend it (i.e. his hymnbook!) to
> every truly pious reader, as a means of raising or

quickening the spirit of devotion; of confirming his faith; of enlivening his hope; and of kindling and increasing his love to God and man. When Poetry thus keeps its place as the handmaid of Piety, it shall attain not a poor perishable wreath, but a crown that fadeth not away."

Anyone interested in enjoying some of the Brethren communion hymns referred to above should consult, the following hymnbooks, among others. Unfortunately several of these selections are published as words only editions; however, usually metrical notations are provided. *The Believers Hymn Book* (with supplement), Published by John Ritchie Limited, Scotland; *Hymns of Light and Love*, published by Echoes of Service, Bath, England; *Hymns of Worship and Remembrance*, published by, Gospel Perpetuating Publishers, Belle Chaise, LA,; or *Christian Worship*, published by Paternoster Press, Exeter, England.

Part 4

Communion and Creed

"Whatever God commands us to do, we are to do. Now God commands, "Do this in remembrance of Me". This, therefore, we are to do, because He commands; whether we find present benefit thereby, or not. But undoubtedly we shall find benefit sooner or later, though perhaps insensibly. We shall be insensibly strengthened, made more fit for the service of God, and more constant in it."

John Wesley

Chapter 14

The Lord's Supper and Christian Theology

It is vital to consider the relationship between our understanding of the Lord's Supper and the great doctrines of our Christian faith. If we discover that this or that view of the Supper is in conflict with the biblical doctrine of the Person and Work of Christ, we shall regard it with suspicion, no matter who its advocates may be.

The Lord's Supper & The Doctrine Of Scripture

The question before us here is, "How does our understanding of the Lord's Supper influence our doctrine of Scripture?" In each of the Synoptic institution narratives, as well as in John chapter 13, we see Jesus acting consistently in the light of Scripture. He is not simply seeing events against the back-ground of Scripture but He is clearly determined that every word of scripture that relates to His Passion shall be fulfilled. This is not at all surprising in the light of our Lord's stated view concerning the authority and focus of Scripture. Here for example, are His own words, *"And the Father who sent Me has Himself testified concerning Me. You have never heard His voice nor seen His form, nor does His word dwell in you. For you do not believe the One He sent. You diligently study the Scriptures because you think that by them you possess eternal life. These are the Scriptures that testify about Me, yet you refuse to come to Me to have life."* (John 5:37-40). And again *"...the Scripture cannot be broken"* (John 10:35; cf. Luke 24:27-44).

This is particularly important in the light of our present inquiry. Speaking of His sense of destiny and of the fulfilling of Scripture we hear Jesus say. *"My appointed time (ho kairos) is here, I am going to celebrate the Passover with My disciples at your house."* (Matt. 26:18; cf. Mark 14:14; Luke 22:11). While He will use the occasion to institute His own Celebration of Remembrance, the Saviour is clearly conforming to traditional Passover practice as prescribed in Scripture (cf. Ex. 12:17-20). He moves under a sense of divine appointment.

Then, as the Supper proceeds Jesus begins to unmask the traitor. Even as He does so, He again sets His words against the background of Scripture: *"The Son of Man will go just as it is written about Him. But woe to the man who betrays the Son of Man!"* (Matt. 26:23). Just what passage Jesus has in mind is made clear in John 13:18: *"I am not referring to all of you; I know those I have chosen. But this is to fulfill the scripture: He who shares My bread has lifted up his heel against Me?"* (see Ps. 41:9). Clearly, He is moving in harmony with Scripture. In a sense He is allowing it to determine His movements.

There are at least two references in Paul's famous passage on the Lord's Supper that suggest his view is also controlled by Scripture (cf. 1 Cor. 10 and 11). The apostle uses two Old Testament illustrations to reinforce his eucharistic ethic. Speaking of the Israelites' lax behaviour, despite their eating divinely provided food and drink, Paul writes, *"Do not be idolaters, as some of them were, as it is written: "The people sat down to eat and drink and got up to indulge in profane revelry"* (1 Cor. 10:7). He has something similar in mind in verse 18 when he asks: *"Do not those who eat the sacrifices participate in the altar?"* He then goes on to say: *"...and I do not want you to be participants with demons. You cannot drink the cup of the Lord and the cup of demons too: you cannot have a part in both the Lord's table and the table of demons."*

It is as though he is saying, "let the Scripture guide and guard your actions, including your behaviour at, and belief about, the Lord's Supper." In 1 Corinthians 11:23 the apostle quite deliberately bases his teaching on a dominical saying. In other words he is asserting that whatever he says about the

Lord's Supper comes directly from the Lord. Here are his familiar words, *"For I received from the Lord what I also passed on to you."* He then quotes the Lord's own words, not as though they constituted a sort of consecration formula, but to underline the fact that his own doctrine of the Lord's Supper is derived from the Lord Himself. Furthermore, as already noted, Paul seems to suggest that the proclaimed Word and the Lord's Supper go together (cf. v. 26).

Paul's association of the Lord's Supper and the proclamation of Scripture, was an idea central to the understanding of the Reformers. For them, a truly evangelical Christian faith will always find its focus in the Word and the Table. The Lord's Supper is explained and authenticated by the Word, while the Word is validated by the Supper and both are authorized by the Lord Himself.

The Lord's Supper & Christology

The question Jesus asked the Pharisees: *"What do you think of Christ?"* This reminds us that there is no more important area of Christian doctrine than Christology (cf. Matt. 22:42). This is especially true in our understanding of the Lord's Supper. Any view of it which is in conflict with New Testament Christology must be abandoned. As John Newton succinctly put it: "You cannot be right in the rest if you do not think rightly of Him." The importance of this becomes apparent when we are faced with the so-called ontological or realistic interpretations of the Lord's Supper, such as transubstantiation and consubstantiation.

The doctrine of transubstantiation suggests that, upon consecration by the priest, the bread and wine, while retaining their "accidents," are changed in substance, into the actual flesh and blood of Christ. Now, however this may be argued philosophically or even from selected, biblical proof texts, the fact remains that it is in conflict with orthodox, New Testament Christology.

If it is true as the Roman Catholic church teaches, that every time and in every place where the "Host" is consecrated, "the whole Christ is contained under each 'species'" (i.e. the bread and the wine) and under every part of each species, then it follows that the infinite, uncreated, eternal, divine Lord Jesus Christ is confined to and contained in certain physical, geographical locations. Such ideas are not only preposterous but plainly in conflict with both Scripture and orthodox Christian belief concerning our Lord's Person (see for example, the Athanasian and Nicene Creeds). If words mean anything, the Almighty Christ who is equal in Godhead, in Glory and in Majesty with the Father, cannot be conceived as "confected" by a mortal man, nor confined to a local sacrament.

Similarly, but for different reasons, the doctrine of consubstantiation also founders upon the rock of biblical Christology. After all, it follows that if Christ's "real, physical and whole presence" is known "in, with and under" the bread and wine, as Luther affirmed, then Christ's humanity must be possessed of the quality of ubiquity or even omnipresence. This of course is in conflict with the biblical view of Christ's real humanity. In fact it begins to sound like a resuscitated docetism (the view that Christ's humanity was not real but only appeared to be so).

According to the New Testament, Christ is at present in heaven as a glorified man. It is not as though His humanity is here or there, or in several places at once. He is wholly and really present at the right hand of God; focus of the adoring hosts of Glory and acting as the One and only Intermediary on behalf of His people (cf. Rom. 8:34; 2 Tim. 2:5). There He will remain until He returns to welcome His waiting people home (Heb. 1:3; 7:26-28; 9:24-28).

Nothing could be plainer than the words of the angelic messengers on Ascension Day, *"'Men of Galilee', they said, 'why do you stand here looking into the sky? This same Jesus, who has been taken from you into heaven, will come back in the same way you have seen Him go into heaven,'"* (Acts 1:11). To attempt to conjure up a literal, physical presence of Christ in the Mass sounds like superstition or magic and is surely to be condemned in the light of Scripture (cf. Rom. 10:6).

On a more positive note, we must recognize that in any meaningful celebration of the Lord's Supper, Christology will hold an important place. Our Lord's words of institution, *"do this in remembrance of Me"* should caution us against becoming obsessed with eucharistic liturgies or even evangelical blessings. The whole intent of the Supper is to remind us of Christ in all the wonder of His glorious Person, and to lead us into a deeper, spiritual fellowship with Himself. Of course, there is always the danger of discussing the question, "How is Christ present?" only to realize too late, like the Emmaus pair, that He really was there by His Spirit, all the time, and we missed Him!

Clearly then, our interpretation of the Lord's Supper while Christ-centered must not deny the reality of His humanity nor the fact of His deity. When Christ became man He did not cease to be God and when He returned to Glory He did not cease to be man. These truths we hold inviolate in faith and practice.

The Lord's Supper & The Doctrine Of Salvation

"'Tis finished:" on the Cross He said,
    In agonies and blood;
    'Tis finished: now He lives to plead,
    Before the face of God.

"'Tis finished: here our souls can rest,
    His work can never fail;
    By Him our Sacrifice and Priest,
    We enter thro' the veil."

James A. Deck (1807-1884)

The Breaking of Bread is above all else, a celebration of Christ, crucified and risen. This is clear from Jesus' own words of institution *"This is My body given for you ...My blood, which is poured out for you."* Paul makes this same point when he writes, *"you proclaim the Lord's death until He comes"*. This remembrance of Christ's death will obviously affect us in many different ways. It will move us to thanksgiving and worship; it will

113

motivate us to live lives of devotion and service; it will also secure us in the knowledge that Christ's work is finished and so our redemption assured.

'The Sacrifice of Mass' is a blatant parody of the New Testament doctrine of the atonement. It was this of course that roused the Reformers. They recognized that in Scripture, the death of Christ on the Cross was not only a sufficient but a final work for the salvation of sinners. As the book of Hebrews puts it: *"The Son is the radiance of God's glory, and the exact representation of His being, sustaining all things by His powerful word. After He had provided purification for sins, He sat down at the right hand of the Majesty in heaven"* (Heb. 1:3).

Several things emerge from this verse which relate to our present topic. First, there is an unequivocal statement of Our Lord's deity. Second, there is reference to His complete and efficacious work. Third, there is a description of His enthronement in heaven, in recognition that His work on earth is done.

It is unfortunate that the Latin Vulgate and translations based on it, misrepresent the original Greek text of this passage by substituting the present participle, *faciens* for the Greek *aorist* participle, *poiesamenos*. Whereas the latter describes a once-for-all, completed action, the former allows for an ongoing process. The seriousness of this mistranslation can be measured from the consequent blasphemous claims made in regard to the Mass. Take the following for example, "And forasmuch as, in this divine sacrifice which is celebrated in the Mass, that same Christ is contained and immolated in an unbloody manner who once offered Himself in a bloody manner on the altar of the cross ...this sacrifice is truly propitiatory...Wherefore not only for the sins... of the faithful who are living, but also for those who are not yet fully purified..."

In case the reader has any doubt regarding the New Testament's teaching concerning, *"the finished work of Christ"*, here is a list of scriptures that will clarify the issue: Mark 10:45; John 19:30; Acts 20:28; Romans 3:24-25; 5:9; 8:3-4; 1 Corinthians 1:23-24; Galatians 3:13; Ephesians 1:7; Colossians 2:14-15; 1 Timothy 2:6; Hebrews 7:27; 9:12,26; 10:12; 1 Peter 3:18.

Any view of the Lord's Supper which sees it as efficacious for salvation or propitiatory, even in the slightest degree, is a plain denial of the New Testament doctrine of salvation. So again we see that our interpretation of the Lord's Supper must be adjudicated by biblical theology.

When we come to the Lord's Supper we come to remember our Saviour; to celebrate His redeeming work and to give thanks for the wonderful benefits secured for us through His all-sufficient sacrifice. While we deny that the Supper, in and of itself, has any saving efficacy, we do not deny its importance and significance. We are always blessed and renewed in remembering our Lord. However, that does not mean that the Lord's Supper is a means of Grace that automatically communicates special grace to those who partake of the emblems. It is a unique occasion of commemoration, not a means of communicating saving grace, as some sacramental views of the Supper appear to suggest.

Salvation and the forgiveness of sins are enjoyed by grace through faith alone (*sola gratia, sola fide*). No work of supererogation nor unbloody sacrifice can add to the finished work of Calvary. The Cross is without alternative and needs no supplement or complement (Rom. 3:23-26; 5:8-9; Eph. 2:8; Tit. 3:4-7).

The Lord's Supper & The Doctrine Of The Holy Spirit

Calvin, reluctant to accept materialistic interpretations of the Eucharist, yet adamantly opposed to Zwinglian commemorationism, made much of the ministry of the Holy Spirit in relation to the Lord's Supper. He described the Spirit as the "internal minister through whose good offices the efficacy of the Supper is conveyed to the communicant."

While rejecting theories of localized deity or ubiquitous humanity, Calvin could still speak of Christ's real presence. In his view, while Christ remained enthroned in heaven, at the Lord's Supper believers were lifted up into fellowship with Him by the ministry of the Holy Spirit. The Supper thus becomes a Means of Grace; a sacramental sign of an inward reality. To miss communion meant forfeiting a unique spiritual experience of feeding on Christ.

Although Scripture is silent about the Holy Spirit's role in the Lord's Supper, there are certainly pointers that suggest He will be involved. For example, in His Upper Room discourse, which was closely associated with His Last Supper, Jesus promises,

> *"But when He, the Spirit of Truth, comes He will guide you into all truth. He will not speak on His own; He will speak only what He hears, and He will tell you what is yet to come. He will bring glory to Me by taking from what is Mine and making it known to you."* (John 16:13-14).

Jesus also implies that the Holy Spirit, His alter ego, will make His presence real to His disciples, although He Himself will be physically removed from them (cf. John 14:18). Those who do not accept Calvin's sacramental view of the Lord's Supper but feel more comfortable with a Zwinglian type of commemoration, nevertheless firmly acknowledge the ministry of the Holy Spirit. In their view there is nothing different about the presence of Christ at the Lord's Supper from His presence on any other occasion when Christians meet together in His name (cf. Matt. 18:20). They would say that it is always the ministry of the Spirit to make Christ real to the believer.

Since He is the Sovereign, eternal Spirit in whose presence there is freedom, He will not be limited by means or occasion, (cf. 2 Cor. 3:17). A proper understanding of biblical pneumatology will teach us that the Spirit's presence will be known in the Church which is His temple (*naos*: 'inner sanctuary'). It is he who incorporated the Church through the Word which He inspired (1 Cor. 2:13; 3:16 , 12:13; 2 Tim. 3:16 and 2 Pet. 1:21).

The Lord' Supper & Eschatology

There is no more important aspect of biblical eschatology in this so-called terminal generation than the blessed hope of Christ's personal return, often referred to as His Parousia (literally: arrival). Yet surprisingly, in a world filled with despair,

Christians generally, seem quite hesitant if not reluctant to share this good news. It is here that the Lord's Supper can be so eloquent and heartening. When we break bread, we not only commemorate Christ's death and resurrection but thoughtfully anticipate His Coming. This is in line with Our Lord's words of institution, and the Bible (see Luke 22: 16-18 and 1 Cor. 11:26).

The Lord's Supper is not to be thought of as an end in itself but rather as a means to an end. While we may debate ad nauseam the manner of Christ's presence in the Eucharist, the great fact to keep in mind is that when Christ returns, we shall no longer need emblems: we shall have Him: faith will give place to sight!

Here again we see how our theology informs our remembrance. Our eschatology will remind us again that joy, not morbidity should characterize a communion service. It warns us against becoming obsessed with prescribed forms and liturgies, while encouraging us to live in hope. Our blessed hope, like the Supper itself, is an incentive to holiness and a call to mission (1 John 3:1-3). Usually a church that believes in and preaches about the Lord's return, will be a place where evangelism and the Lord's Supper are given due prominence.

The Lord's Supper & The Doctrine Of The Church

Scripture offers a close link between the doctrine of the church and teaching about the ordinances. It is not surprising therefore to discover that in most volumes on Systematic theology, baptism and the Lord's Supper are dealt with under the general heading of ecclesiology. This connection is obvious in the book of Corinthians. For example, *"And is not the bread that we break a participation (koinōnia) in the body of Christ? Because there is one loaf we who are many, are one body, for we all partake of the one loaf."* (1 Cor. 10:16).

The apostle combines two metaphors here: loaf and body in order to stress the ideas of unity in variety, and variety in unity (cf. 1 Cor. 12:13-16). Just as many grains make up one loaf and many members constitute one body, so the great variety of Christian believers forms the one true Church of which the

Lord Jesus is the Head. Paul makes this point again in his following chapter where he suggests that the cliquishness of the Corinthian church is really a denial of the truth of the Christian unity which is given visible expression in the Lord's Supper. Listen to his words: *"For anyone who eats and drinks without recognizing the body of the Lord, eats and drinks judgment on himself,"* (1 Cor. 11:29). These strong words show how committed Paul was to the idea that the Lord's Supper is, or at least should be, an eloquent and visible statement about Christian unity. Clearly, in this context, recognizing or discerning the body, refers primarily to the mystical body of Christ (i.e. the Church) rather than His physical body as symbolized by the bread, that latter fact could hardly be missed.

What are the practical corollaries of the apostle's teaching in terms of our celebration of the Lord's Supper? First, it is clear that the Supper is a congregational rather than a private, personal event. While we each come to the Lord's Table with his or her own basket of first fruits, we come together with our brothers and sisters in Christ (cf. Deut. 26:1-11). In each instance where the Breaking of Bread is mentioned in the New Testament, we have Christians coming together and celebrating together (cf. Acts 2:42, 46; 20:7 or 11;17, 20).

This congregational aspect, implied in the very word 'Communion,' should warn us against isolationism and sectarianism on the one hand, and sacerdotalism on the other. The idea of an intercessory priest, celebrating the Lord's Supper alone or on behalf of other Christians, is alien to New Testament teaching about both the Church and the Lord's Supper. By the same token, a Christian who chooses to break bread privately because he feels unable to fellowship with other believers, for whatever reason, is denying the very spirit of the Lord's Supper.

A true understanding of biblical ecclesiology will help to guard us against any precept or practice that separates or excludes believers from the Table of the Lord. To decide arbitrarily who shall and who shall not break bread with us, not only gives the lie to the truth of the oneness of the Body of Christ, but denies the very spirit of Christ Himself (cf. Rom.

THE LORD'S SUPPER & CHRISTIAN THEOLOGY

15:7). The Lord's Supper is certainly one place where we should, make every effort to *"keep the unity of the Spirit through the bond of peace."* (Eph. 4:3).

Another important aspect of Christian fellowship associated with the Lord's Supper is the call to give practical expression to Christian love. After all, it was as they prepared to eat the Last Supper that the Lord washed His disciples' feet. One of the great blessings of Early Church meetings was that they were held in the believers' homes. This would encourage and help cultivate the gift of hospitality, something sadly overlooked in many churches today (cf. Heb. 13:1-2; 1 Pet. 4:9).

Finally, remembering that each member of the Church is endued with at least one spiritual gift, we should seek to reflect this in our celebration of the Lord's Supper. It should prompt each of us to come prepared to express our appreciation of Christ, whether audibly or inaudibly.

The Lord's Supper & Christian Living

As we have already observed, there is an essential link between the Christian doctrine of holy living and our celebration of the Lord's Supper. At least two things are necessary in any true worship, sincerity and morality. Any teaching about the Lord's Supper which presents it merely as a procedure to be gone through, while having no bearing on our day to day lifestyle must be regarded as suspect (cf. John 4:23-24). While there is no saving or sanctifying merit in taking communion and certainly no prophylactic value, as is sometimes imagined, it is a solemn and serious occasion with strong ethical prerequisites.

Two things are wisely kept in mind when we come together to remember our Lord. First, that we all come as *"sinners saved by grace."* Second, that we are, *"...a chosen people, a royal priesthood, a holy nation, a people belonging to God that (we) may declare the praises of Him who called* [us] *out of darkness into His wonderful light."* (1 Pet. 2:9). Let us beware lest, *"having a form of godliness we deny its power"* (2 Tim. 3:5). How sad to go through the motions only to be told, *"it is not the Lord's Supper you eat,"* (1 Cor. 11:20).

Part 5

A Brief Historical Review

Question: "What are the sacraments?"

Answer: "They are the visible holy signs and seals instituted by God in order that by their use He may the more fully disclose and seal to us the promise of the Gospel, namely, that because of the one sacrifice of Christ accomplished on the Cross He graciously grants to us the forgiveness of sins and eternal life.

(Question 66, *the Heidelberg Catechism,* 1563).

Chapter 15

The Early Centuries

Early Christian Teaching

Our primary concern in this book is with biblical teaching about the Lord's Supper, and its contemporary interpretation and practice. However, it is important that we take a very brief look at the historical development of eucharistic doctrines. Our purpose in this is at least three-fold. First, it will alert us to the hidden dangers that lie in our path, theologically speaking. Second, it will help us sort the wood from the trees, so to speak; to see which things are essential and which are optional; which are scriptural and which are merely traditional. Third, it will help us appreciate the primacy of this ordinance in the life of the Christian Church, across the almost two millennia of its history. We shall discover that for all their divergent interpretations, Christians have always recognized the spiritual necessity of the Lord's Supper and have encouraged each other in its regular observance. It has helped them to find focus in their worship; discern their identity; and drawn them closer together, particularly in times of pressure and persecution. In this brief overview, after a look at the earliest centuries, we shall focus more on teaching about the Lord's Supper from the time of Wycliffe. This section of our book is not intended to be other than introductory. Others have written much more extensively on the history of the Lord's Supper and can be read to profit.

The Primitive Church

We have already seen that the New Testament churches

were quite informal and unstructured in their understanding and celebration of the Lord's Supper. In fact, due to the scant notice given this Christian ordinance in the Book of Acts and the Epistles, we actually know very little about the Primitive Church's eucharistic traditions and practices. What seems clear is that in New Testament times Christian congregations whether small or large, met regularly, generally on the first day of the week, to break bread in remembrance of the Lord Jesus Christ. They were evidently not so concerned about interpretation and orthodoxy as they were to give visible expression to their obedience to Christ and their spiritual union with each other. No doubt, much of their thinking about the Lord's Supper would have been coloured by their understanding and experience of the Passover meal, this would be specially true of the strong Jewish element in the early churches. After all, Jesus instituted His Supper on the occasion of a Passover meal and even included some Paschal references.

It would appear that there were two or three main planks in primitive eucharistic tradition. The Lord's Supper was viewed as an active, memorial drama of Christ's sacrifice and victory; as a practical expression of Christian fellowship and as a proclamation of the Church's blessed hope. The Lord's Supper called for self examination, personal piety, and the practical acceptance of all who were fellow members of Christ's body.

The early Christians were not concerned to formulate theological dogma about the manner in which Christ's presence was to be expected or experienced at Communion. They did not worry about such things as real presence, spiritual presence or local presence, nor did they quibble about, memorials or means of grace. By the same token, they were evidently not inhibited by this or that prescribed, liturgical order nor by the absence of qualified celebrants. Such debates and distractions were left for later generations. As we move on from the New Testament period we shall soon discover all kinds of diversionary tendencies.

The Apostolic Fathers

The Didachē c. A.D. 100

It is in such non-canonical, early Christian writings as the *Didachē* ("The teaching of the apostles" to give it its full title) that we see the first evidence of deviation, some might call it development from the Early Church's teaching about the Lord's Supper. Two passages from this document of the sub-apostolic era are relevant to our subject and worth quoting at length.

The first refers to what is called, 'the eucharistic thanksgiving'; the second, to a gathering 'on the Lord's own day'.

> (i) "First, as regards the cup: we give Thee thanks, o our Father, for the holy vine of Thy son David, which Thou madest known unto us through Thy Son Jesus... Then as regards the broken bread: we give Thee thanks, o our Father, for the life and knowledge which Thou didst make known unto us through Thy Son Jesus... As this broken bread was scattered upon the mountains and being gathered together became one, so may Thy Church be gathered together... but let no one eat or drink of this eucharistic thanksgiving, but they that have been baptized into the name of the Lord..." (Paragraph 9).[11]

> (ii) "And on the Lord's own day gather yourselves together and break bread and give thanks, first confessing your transgressions, that your sacrifice (*thusia*) may be pure... And let no man having his dispute with his fellow, join your assembly until they have been reconciled, that your sacrifice is that which was spoken of by the Lord. 'In every place and at every time offer Me a pure sacrifice (*thusia*); for I am a great King saith the Lord, and My name is wonderful among the nations.' " (Paragraph 14)[12]

---

11 J.B.Lightfoot, *The Apostolic Fathers*. London: Macmillan,1893, p.232.
12 Ibid. p.234

The former of these passages, *Paragraph 9*, is interesting for several reasons. First, it suggests an unusual order, the cup before the bread. Second, there is its interpretation of the loaf as symbolical of the church. And third, it views baptism as a prerequisite for Communion.

Paragraph 14 is also important in that it is usually cited as the earliest evidence in support of a sacrificial interpretation of the Lord's Supper. However, this is suspect for the following reasons. First, why is it so far separated from paragraph 9? Secondly, it is not clear whether this paragraph is referring to the Eucharist, or to the early Christian communal meal usually known as the *Agapē*. It seems more likely that it is the latter. In which case, as noted elsewhere, the pure sacrifice points to a spiritual sacrifice of praise such as is envisaged in Hebrews 13:15, not to the Eucharist, viewed as a sacrifice (cf. Mal.1:11).

The Apologists

Justin Martyr c. A.D. 100 – 165

One of Justin Martyr's most valuable contributions to our understanding of second century teaching concerning the Lord's Supper is his following description of a typical celebration :

> "The memoirs of the apostles or the writings of the prophets are read aloud as time permits. The 'president' then delivers a sermon exhorting obedience to what has been read. Then follow prayers to the same end; on behalf of all Christians everywhere, which all present take part in, standing. At the conclusion of these prayers they salute one another with a kiss. The bread and cup are brought to the president; he takes them and offers up praise and glory to the Father of the universe through the Name of the Son and the Holy Spirit, and, to the best of his power makes a long thanksgiving because God has deigned to bestow these things upon us. All the people present express assent to this thanksgiving by the Hebrew word, 'Amen'.

> Then those who are called 'deacons' distribute the bread and the cup for which thanksgiving has thus been offered, to all present, and carry a portion also to those who are absent."[13]

Justin is sometimes charged with holding a kind of incipient doctrine of transubstantiation and with being unduly sacramentalist, in his view of the Lord's Supper. He certainly uses questionable language when he writes, "We have been taught that the food which is blessed by the prayer of His Word, and from which our blood and flesh by transmutation are nourished, is the flesh and blood of that Jesus who was made flesh" (Apologia 1:66).[14] He speaks of the Eucharist as "a sacrifice of thanksgiving" and, like the *Didachē*, sees it as a fulfillment of Malachi's *"pure sacrifice"* (cf. Mal. 1:11) (Dialogue 41). In a further, rather fanciful, interpretive comment regarding an Old Testament ceremony, Justin sees the offering of fine flour as a type of the bread of the Eucharist (cf. Lev. 14).

The Epistles of Ignatius c. A.D. 115

Although there is very little about the Lord's Supper in the seven famous letters Ignatius wrote en route for his martyrdom, two references are significant. Both point in the direction of a developing sacerdotalism. In his letter to the Ephesians Ignatius writes, "If anyone be not within the precinct of the altar, he lacketh the bread (of God)" (Paragraph 5).[15]

He is even more specific when he writes to the Philadelphians, "Be ye careful therefore to observe one eucharist (for there is one flesh of our Lord Jesus Christ and one cup unto union in His blood) that whatsoever ye do, ye may do it after God" (Epistle to the Philadelphians', Paragraph 4).

---

13   A.R. Witham,. The History of the Christian Church; Rivington's London, p.81-82.

14   Ibid. p. 81.

15   J.B. Lightfoot, Apostolic Fathers p.154.

Irenaeus c. A.D. 130 – 202.

Irenaeus, who became Bishop of Lyons c. A.D. 170, had known Polycarp who in turn was a follower of the apostle John, and therefore, could claim a link with the apostolic age. He seems to have developed much of his eucharistic doctrine in the course of his rebuttal of Gnosticism. This may account to a certain degree, for some of his rather confusing statements. For example, like other apologists, Irenaeus taught that the Eucharist was the "pure sacrifice" foretold in Malachi 1:11. His famous statement says, "The Jews cannot make such an offering for they do not have the Word who is offered to God" (*Fragments* xxxvi).

This certainly sounds like the later, doctrine of the Mass. However, in Irenaeus' defense it is sometimes noted that his words may have been taken out of context. Furthermore, although Irenaeus speaks of the bread and wine as, "offerings to God", he denied they had any meritorious significance. In fact he describes them as "gifts of creation which are used at the Lord's Supper simply as means of celebration."

There is also evidence that Irenaeus taught that through the invocation of the divine name over the elements, the divine *Logos* becomes mysteriously connected with them. He suggested that the loaf is no longer common bread but "Eucharist" and that through receiving it the Christian's body is "no longer corruptible but has hope of resurrection to eternity" (*Against Heresies*, IV.18).

On the other hand, Irenaeus insisted that the bread and wine are to be viewed merely as a thank offering. This seeming confusion of ideas might well be resolved if we had more precise information about the context of his words.

Tertullian c. A.D. 160 – 215

Tertullian (by training a lawyer) was a Christian controversialist and apologist from North Africa. He was a prolific writer and not surprisingly, held quite strong views on the Lord's Supper. While he saw it as a fulfillment of Malachi's *"pure sacrifice,"* he denied that the bread and wine were the same as, or in any way contained the Lord's body and blood. He distinguished between the symbol (*sacramentum*) and that which is symbolized (*res sacramenti*).

In his treatise on prayer, Tertullian seems to recognize that the sacrifices Christians offer are not material but spiritual ones. He writes, "We are the true priests who worshipping in the Spirit, do in spirit, sacrifice prayer suitable to God and acceptable." (*de Oratione XXVII*).

Origen c. A.D. 185 – 254

Origen who was one of the first genuinely biblical scholars, rejected the more sacerdotal, sacramental tendencies of his contemporaries. He emphasized the truth that the bread and wine were merely symbolical emblems of the body and blood of Christ. For him the emblems were a means whereby the simple Christian would think about the great foundational fact of their faith: the sacrifice of the Saviour.

Origen writes, "It is not what enters the mouth that sanctifies a man - even though simpler folk may think that what is called, 'the Lord's bread sanctifies'". It would appear that Origen was essentially what might later be called, a commemorationist.

Cyprian c. A.D. 200 – 258

Cyprian the famous, martyr bishop of Carthage in North Africa, is usually regarded as the first of the early church fathers who specifically interpreted the Lord's Supper as a 'sacrifice'. What he actually said was, "His passion is the offering that we make." This is not surprising coming from Cyprian, particularly in light of his strict ecclesiastical opinions. He held a very conservative view of the clergy, seeing them as mediatorial priests, serving under a monarchical episcopate.

As with other early Fathers, Cyprian's language regarding the Eucharist, tends to be vague if not confused and equivocal. It may well be that his language is coloured due to his dispute with the Aquarii, a strange sect so named because of their insistence on the use of water rather than wine at the Lord's Supper! Opinions are often overstated in the heat of debate, than in careful discussion.

Augustine of Hippo c. A.D. 354 – 430

Augustine who became Bishop of Hippo in Numidia, North Africa, has been described as the greatest of the Latin fathers. He is often viewed as a direct link between Paul and the Reformation. Typically, his evangelical, biblical approach is seen in his understanding of the Lord's Supper. While rejecting the materialistic interpretation of Cyprian, Augustine goes further than the commemorationist views of Origen.

In stressing his view that the Lord's Supper while not communicating the actual body and blood of Christ, was rather, a means of Grace, Augustine is sometimes quite ambivalent. On the one hand he taught that at the Supper the bread and wine remain what they appear to be to the human, physical senses "simply bread and wine". Yet in one of his famous sermons he says, "…that bread which you see on the altar, consecrated through the Word of God, is the Body of Christ; that cup yes indeed, what the cup contains, consecrated by the Word of God, is the Blood of Christ" (Sermon 227).

Augustine taught that the Lord's Supper was not only a memorial but a "visible word". For him the bread and wine were, *signa visibilia invisibilis gratiae* ("visible signs of invisible grace"). He suggested that Lord's Supper was a sacred sign or pledge of the death of Christ, yet made a clear distinction between the partaking of the elements and the spiritual experience of the communicant. This is how he put it, "It is not that which is seen that feeds, but that which is believed" (Sermon 112:50.) For Augustine, the key lies in the perception of faith on the part of the communicant. Discerning between the invisible, spiritual reality and the visible, material symbol is essential. Clearly such ideas laid the foundation for much of the Reformation teaching about the Lord's Supper.

Despite the great influence Augustine had on the teaching

of the Reformers, his views on the Lord's Supper were not generally espoused by his immediate successors. There were reasons for this, one in particular being the Medieval Catholic Church's attitude to Scripture. As the official Church moved into the "Dark Ages," superstition and established ecclesiastical tradition took precedence over biblical revelation.

With this shift in the ground of authority came the increasing dependence of the ordinary Christian on the power-hungry, corrupt and, for the most part, scripturally ignorant clergy. As the imagined authority of priests to consecrate the elements and "confect" the body and blood of Christ was accepted, so the spiritual understanding of the Lord's Supper declined. More and more emphasis was placed on so-called materialistic, ontological views of the Lord's Supper and eventually, Christendom was saddled with the doctrine of transubstantiation

It becomes obvious even from these, brief historical glimpses, that the official, post-apostolic Church, perhaps better called "Christendom" quickly departed from the New Testament understanding and celebration of the Lord's Supper. This was all part and parcel of the development of the ecclesiastical hierarchy with its unscriptural pretensions; its political entanglements and its sacerdotalism. During the following centuries, properly described as "the Dark Ages," the story did not get any better but rather grew worse, at least in official church circles. The Lord's Supper became shrouded in all kinds of superstitions and idolatrous practices. However, we shall not concern ourselves with these things further, but move forward to a consideration of the more enlightened times of the Reformation, heralded as they were by the insight and ministry of John Wycliffe.

Chapter 16

John Wycliffe's Teaching On The Lord's Supper

Three foundational truths recovered in the Reformation were, the doctrine of Justification through faith; the authority and sufficiency of Scripture, and the simplicity of the Lord's Supper. Clearly these all go hand in hand. In this chapter we are particularly concerned with the development of eucharistic theology in England, through the influence of such men as John Wycliffe and Thomas Cranmer. Later, we will look at the European theologians' understanding of the Lord's Supper.

John Wycliffe, 1325 – 1384

Wycliffe was a remarkable man by any standard. He went up to Oxford from his home in Yorkshire, while still in his teens, and quickly developed into one of the brightest intellects of his day. Coupled with his clear-mindedness and sincere devotion to Christ, was a singular appreciation of the peerless authority and truth of Scripture. He was at least a century ahead of his time in his understanding of the teachings of Scripture, particularly in relation to the Lord's Supper. He well deserves the title, "Morning Star of the Reformation".

So profound was Wycliffe's influence and so disturbing to the Roman Catholic Church that dominated England in his day, that just over forty years after his death, that church had his bones exhumed, and burned. His ashes were then scattered on the River Swift at Lutterworth where he had ministered.

Surprising though it may seem, it was after his expulsion from the University in 1378 and his return to the Rectory at Lutterworth, that Wycliffe sowed his most fertile seeds of reformation. On the one hand, he encouraged the translation of the Bible, from Latin, into the English vernacular. On the other, he developed his doctrine of the Lord's Supper. It was in these years, despite deteriorating health, that he produced several very important works, including his *On the Truth of Holy Scripture* (1378); *Confession* (1381) and, most significantly for our present study, *de Eucharistia* (1380) and *Trialogus* (1384). Wycliffe's effectiveness was multiplied by his recruitment and training of a band of followers, known as the Lollards. Their task was to go forth to preach the Gospel and expound the Scriptures in English.

Wycliffe's careful rejection of the doctrine of transubstantiation proceeded along several lines. He suggested that such teaching was unreasonable, unscriptural, idolatrous and lacking in ancient historical precedent. First, as to its unreasonableness, Wycliffe wrote: "Since transubstantiation is so contrary to the senses it is unworthy of God, since without good reason, it not only destroys guiltless existence but it puts confusion on that intellect which He has implanted in our nature" (*Trialogus* pp. 145 ff.). [16]

Wycliffe rejected Thomas Aquinas' argument about the bread retaining its "accidents" while being changed as to its substance. He becomes quite satirical about this when he writes: "Mice, however, have an innate knowledge of the fact, that the substance of bread is retained, as at the first; but these unbelievers have no such knowledge, since they know not what bread or what wine are consecrated, except they have seen the act of consecration performed." (*Trialogus* p. 142). [17]

Second, as to the unscripturalness of the doctrine of transubstantiation, Wycliffe's argument went in part, as follows. He pointed out that the apostle Paul spoke about *"the bread*

---

16 D.B. Knox, *The Lord's Supper from Wycliffe to Cranmer*, Exeter, Paternoster Press. p.12.

17 Ibid. p.12.

which we break" (1 Cor, 10 and 11), not about bread which has been changed into Christ's body. He writes, "It is impossible to believe that Paul would have been so careless as to frequently to have called this sacrament bread, and not by its real name, had he known that it was not bread, but an accident without a subject." (*Trialogus* p. 140).[18]

Third, Wycliffe's most scathing attack on transubstantiation was in his rejection of it because it encouraged the laity to practice idolatry. He ridiculed the idea of the priest having the power to "make Christ's body." Wycliffe complained that such idolatry was worse than paganism which for all its idol making, still recognized that its idols were made of substances such as gold, wood and stone.

Fourth, Wycliffe's further argument against transubstantiation was that it was only of comparatively recent origin. He showed that it was not in keeping with the early patristic teaching about the Lord's Supper. He pointed out that even as late as A.D. 1059, Berengar of Tours had been required to confess as orthodoxy, "that the same bread and wine which were placed before the Mass upon the altar, remain after the consecration both as sacrament and as the Lord's body."[19] In typically uncompromising language Wycliffe continues, "As late as the eleventh century after Christ's resurrection, therefore, no dogma of transubstantiation was known; Satan has been bound for the first thousand years, and only thereafter had begun to work actively in spreading error, with the Pope as Antichrist."[20]

Apart from his attacks on the doctrine of transubstantiation, which may appear rather negative, Wycliffe has some positive things to say about the Lord's Supper. Indeed, so clear was his teaching on this subject that his influence was felt beyond the shores of England and left its stamp on all later Reformation eucharistic theology.

In order to appreciate Wycliffe's understanding of the Lord's

18 Ibid. p.11.
19 G.H.Parker, *The Morning Star*, Paternoster Pressm Exeter, England. 1965. p.41, footnote 1
20 Ibid. footnote 2

Supper, we need to outline its salient features.

First, regarding Christ's words of institution, *"this is My body"*, Wycliffe explains that this must be understood sacramentally or figuratively.[21] "Just as Christ called John the Baptist, 'Elijah' without suggesting that he ceased to be anything that he substantially was before; and just as seven cows are called 'seven years' in Genesis 41; in similar fashion, speaking of literal bread, Christ could say, *'this is My body'"*. As Wycliffe puts it, "You will meet with such modes of expression constantly in Scripture. Now all such expressions show that the thing (*res*) of the subject is ordained by God to be the thing of the predicate." (*Trialogos* p.148).[22]

Second, Wycliffe taught that while the bread of the Eucharist was indeed Christ's body, it was so, not in substance or essence but only, "virtually, spiritually and sacramentally". For him there was no sense in which the literal, physical body of Christ could be anywhere else but in Heaven. Again, to cite Wycliffe's own words, "It is not to be understood that the body of Christ descends to the host in any Church where it is being consecrated but remains above the skies, stable and unmoved" (*Trialogus* p. 132). [23]

If he had been asked to explain what happened to the bread of the Eucharist, after consecration, Wycliffe's answer was that, both the bread and wine "remain substantially as well as in their accidents, alongside the sacramental Body of Christ". This is what is known as Wycliffe's doctrine of Remanence.

A further aspect of his teaching was his so-called "receptionist" view of the Eucharist. This describes his doctrine that, contrary to the *ex opere operato* view of the Tridentine theologians (1545-63) that whoever received the Mass received Christ; he insisted that Christ is received in the Eucharist only through the faith of the participant. As Wycliffe puts it, "Spiritual receiving of the body of Christ does not consist in bodily receiving the consecrated host but in the feeding of the soul out of the fruitful

---

21   D.B. Knox , p.26
22   cited by Knox - p.15
23   ibid. p.16

faith according to which our spirit is nourished in the Lord." (*de Eucharistia* 1:15).

In answer to the question, "how is Christ present in the Eucharist?" John Wycliffe would have replied that he is present spiritually and is discerned to be so by the eye of faith alone. Here are his own words, "we do not see the body of Christ in that sacrament with the bodily eye but only through the faith of the participant" (*de Eucharistia* 1:7). [24]

We should note two other emphases of Wycliffe's eucharistic doctrine here. First, there is his insistence on the spiritual nature of Christian sacrifice; and second, the necessity of piety in the celebrant. In the first of these emphases he was the heir of the Early Fathers but in the second, he was a pioneer.

Wycliffe, while rejecting the idea of the sacrifice of Christ in the Mass, is clear in his understanding that there are, *"spiritual sacrifices, acceptable to God through Jesus Christ"* (1 Pet. 2:5). He expresses it well in de Eucharistia when he writes: "The true worship of God is not in rites and ceremonies or in the adoration of the host, but in the preaching of God's goodness in Christ and in thanksgiving for this. The sacrifice of the Mass consists of praise and thanksgiving for Christ's death" (*de Eucharistia* 1:14). He goes even further and suggests that there are more important things than celebrating the Eucharist, whether for priest or layman. Here again are his words, "The layman, mindful of the body of Christ in heaven, more efficaciously and in a better manner than this priest who performs the sacrament, yet with equal truth (but in another manner) causes the body of Christ to be with him!" (*de Eucharistia* 4:38). By insisting on the necessity of holiness in the life of the celebrant at the Lord's Supper, Wycliffe is pioneering.

The Roman Catholic church taught that the Mass was efficacious "in virtue of the sacramental act itself, and not in virtue of the acts or disposition of the recipient, or of the worthiness of the minister". Wycliffe rejected this opinion completely and taught that the condition of the celebrating minister certainly had a direct bearing on the sacrament. He writes, "since the

---

24   ibid. p.17

host is a sign amongst other things of the union of Christ with the church, it is more efficacious as a sign of this when it is consecrated by a man who is himself in union with Christ" (*de Eucharistia* 4:38). [25]

This stress on the importance of piety in the life of the ministers of the Church was certainly necessary as is evident from the condition of the clergy in Wycliffe's day and indeed since. It is worth noting that this was not simply a matter of theory with Wycliffe but a matter of practical necessity. It was for this reason, among others, that he insisted on exemplary Christian conduct and righteous living, among his followers, the Lollards.

In concluding this chapter, we may say that despite his sometimes difficult expressions and use of the sacramental idiom of his day, Wycliffe was, in the fullest sense, the father of the eucharistic teaching of the English side of the Reformation. The teaching of the Church of England, regarding the Lord's Supper, particularly as expressed in Article 28 of the Thirty Nine Articles, is the direct legacy of this truly visionary man of God.

---

25   ibid

Chapter 17

English Eucharistic Theology After Wycliffe

The conservative, Catholic element which was to dominate to the English Church for the next century and a half following the death of Wycliffe, was determined by all means, to stamp out what was dubbed "Lollard teaching". The particular target of this attack was Wycliffe's view of the Eucharist with its doctrine of remanence. Since the Church was so powerful and the clergy so numerous, anything that threatened its hold over the minds of the common people was suspect and styled "heresy". What could be more threatening to a priest's authority in the eyes of a superstitious populace than to question his imagined ability "to confect Christ" in the Mass? Just how bitter this ecclesiastically instigated attack on Wycliffe's teaching was, can be judged not only from the fanatical exhumation and desecration of his corpse in 1428, but from the passing of the infamous statute, *de heretico comburendo* ("concerning the burning of heretics") in 1401. This statute, which incidentally, has never been repealed, proved to be the license for the burning of multitudes of godly Christians. Included among these heroes of the faith were such men as, William Sawtre (1401); John Badby (1410); William Sweeting (1511); James Brewster (1511); Thomas Man (1518); John Lambert (1538); Thomas Bilney (1531); John Frith (1533); William Tyndale (1535); Hugh Latimer (1555); Thomas Ridley (1555); and Thomas Cranmer (1556).

Despite this determined, diabolical effort by the official Church to stamp out Wycliffe's biblical doctrine of the Lord's Supper, in favour of its own superstitions, the truth survived.

Wycliffe's views not only survived in England during the fifteenth century but were enthusiastically embraced by the European Reformers as well, particularly the Swiss. We shall consider this in our next chapter.

Thomas Cranmer, 1489 – 1556

Although Wycliffe's view of the Lord's Supper had been kept alive both in England and in Europe throughout the fifteenth century, it did not really come back into prominence in England until the middle of the sixteenth century. Its revival was effected thanks largely to Thomas Cranmer who, as Archbishop of Canterbury, set about the task of putting into writing various ancient English liturgies, none more famous than his, *Book of Common Prayer* (1549). Cranmer came into prominence during the reign of Henry VIII, who appointed him Prelate in 1532. He survived the next fifteen years, despite the King's erratic and sometimes dangerous behavior, largely because of his popularity, moderation and personal integrity. When Henry VIII died in 1547 all England must have breathed a sigh of relief, especially those who had prayed and worked for the reformation of the Church. Upon the accession of the boy King, Edward VI, things began to change for the better. This was due not so much to the king but to some of his mentors, including Cranmer. Unfortunately, the respite from Catholicism was short-lived, since Edward VI reigned only nine years and was succeeded in 1553 by his sister, "Bloody Mary". However, the light of truth once shining, was not to be extinguished, for all the savagery and fanaticism of Mary and her Catholic cohorts.

In one of those happy coincidences of history, during Edward's short reign, several things came together. On the one hand, the movement for religious reform had grown stronger and several bishops who had been removed from their seats as a result of Henry VIII's, *Acts of Six Articles*, in 1539, were back and ready to lend their support. On the other, Cranmer's literary and liturgical skills were honed and available. Surprisingly, even during the reign of Henry VIII in 1533, Cranmer had already written and brought into public use, his English Litany, based largely on well known and loved medieval liturgies. Its "prot-estant" flavour was made more palatable because of Cranmer's literary skills. It was not however until 1549 that Cranmer's Prayer Book in the English vernacular was published. Styled to some degree on similar European liturgies, the English Prayer Book was given a mixed reception. It was hated by the Catholics especially because, by the Act of Uniformity of 1549, it replaced the Mass as the legal order of worship. At the same time it was disliked by some of the Reformers because it retained too much sacerdotalism. The *Prayer Book* was revised in 1552 to accommo-date a more reformed point of view. With the notable exception of the reign of Mary (1553-1558), who rejected it and reinstated the Mass, the *Prayer Book* liturgy has survived in regular use until today.

Our particular interest in Cranmer's *Prayer Book* here, is in its teaching about Communion. The wording is important not only as it reflects Cranmer's views, which eventually cost him his life in 1556, but also as it reflects the official findings of the Reformed wing of the Church of England. These findings were stated most clearly by Archbishop Cranmer and Bishop Ridley in a debate convened in the House of Lords in December 1548. The purpose of which, surprisingly, was to discover whether "bread be in the sacrament after the consecration or not."

Several things emerge from Cranmer's statements during that great debate. First, he clearly rejected the doctrine of tran-substantiation by stating, "our faith is not to believe Him to be in the bread and wine, but that He is in heaven." And, secondly, he declared his view of "double eating" by saying: "They be two things, to eat the substance and to eat the body of Christ. The eating of the body is to dwell in Christ, and this may be though a man never taste the sacrament. All men eat not the body in the sacrament". For whatever reason, Cranmer revised his communion liturgy in his 1552 Prayer Book. One significant change was in the words to be spoken by the minister when he administered the elements. The 1549 liturgy read, "The Body of our Lord Jesus Christ, which was given for thee, preserve thy body and soul into everlasting life". In the 1552 version, the fol-lowing sentence was added, "Take and eat this in remembrance that Christ died for thee, and feed on Him in thy heart by faith, with thanksgiving".

Some suggest Cranmer revised his liturgy because he was influenced by the Swiss theologian, Martin Bucer's criticism of the 1549 liturgy in his book *Censura*, published in 1551. Others believe, he did it in order to make it clear that, although he was using accepted ecclesiastical idiom, he rejected the Catholic doctrine of real presence, in favour of a sacramental view. There are a number of references in Cranmer's *Prayer Book* which have a bearing on our present study. For example, in the introduction to the Lord's Supper of which he also called, "Holy Communion", there is a clear reflection of Wycliffe's receptionist views. It reads, "And if any of those be an open and notorious evil liver, or have done any wrong to his neighbours by word or deed, so that the Congregation be thereby offended... he presume not to come to the Lord's Table, until he have openly declared himself to have truly repented and amended his former naughty life...".[26]

A further note in these introductory paragraphs suggests a less formal approach than that in the Mass. Reference is made to the "Table at the Communion time having a fair white linen cloth upon it". There is no suggestion of an altar or sacrifice, although strangely enough, the celebrant is still called, the priest.

The end notes of the common liturgy (in the *Book of Common Prayer*) are also revealing. For example, it is made clear that there is nothing special about the bread that is to be used for Communion. The note reads "and to take away all occasion of dissension and superstition...it shall suffice that the Bread be such as is usual to be eaten...". In a final paragraph, the custom of kneeling to receive Communion is condemned. This so-called, "Black Rubric" reads,

" It is hereby declared, that thereby (kneeling) no adoration is intended, or ought to be done, either unto the Sacramental Bread or Wine there bodily received, or unto any Corporal Presence of Christ's natural Flesh and Blood. For the Sacramental Bread and

---

26   The order of the administration of the Lord's Supper, or Holy Communion, *The Book of Common Prayer.*

Wine remain still in their very natural substances, and therefore may not be adored; (for that were Idolatry, to be abhorred of all faithful Christians); and the natural Body and Blood of our Saviour Christ are in Heaven and not here; it being against the truth of Christ's natural Body to be at one time in more places than one." [27]

One other section of the Prayer Book having a bearing on our subject, and reflecting the work of Cranmer is known as, *Articles of Religion*, (commonly called the *Thirty Nine Articles*). Now, although these Articles were only formally agreed upon during the reign of Queen Elizabeth I, in 1562, it is generally understood that in large measure they reflect the earlier *Forty Two Articles*, published in the reign of Edward VI, in 1553,which were almost certainly the work of Cranmer and Ridley. The relevant articles, (form the concluding paragraphs of the *Book of Common Prayer*) read as follow:

Article XXVIII: Of The Lord's Supper

"The Supper of the Lord is not only a sign of the love that Christians ought to have among themselves one to another; but rather is a Sacrament of our Redemption by Christ's death: insomuch that to such as rightly, worthily, and with faith, receive the same, the Bread which we break is a partaking of the Body of Christ; and likewise the Cup of Blessing is a partaking of the Blood of Christ.

"Transubstantiation, (or the change of the substance of Bread and Wine) in the Supper of the Lord, cannot be proved by holy Writ; but is repugnant to the plain words of Scripture, overthroweth the nature of the Sacrament, and hath given occasion to many superstitions.

"The Body of Christ is given, taken, and eaten, in the Supper, only after an heavenly and spiritual manner. And the means whereby the Body of Christ is received and eaten in the Supper is faith. The Sacrament of the Lord's Supper was not by Christ's ordinance reserved, carried about, lifted up, or worshipped."

---

27   Ibid. endnote

Article xxxix: Of The Wicked Which Eat Not The Body Of Christ In The Use Of The Lord's Supper

"The Wicked, and such as be void of a lively faith, although they do carnally and visibly press with their teeth (as Saint Augustine saith) the Sacrament of the Body and Blood of Christ, yet in no wise are they partakers of Christ; but rather, to their condemnation, do eat and drink the sign or Sacrament of so great a thing."

Article xxx: Of Both Kinds

"The Cup of the Lord is not to be denied to the lay-people: for both the parts of the Lord's Sacrament, by Christ's ordinance and commandment, ought to be ministered to all Christian men alike."

Article xxxi: Of The One Oblation Of Christ Finished Upon The Cross

"The Offering of Christ once made is that perfect redemption, propitiation, and satisfaction, for all the sins of the whole world, both original and actual; and there is none other satisfaction for sin, but that alone. Wherefore the sacrifices of Masses, in the which it was commonly said, that the Priest did offer Christ for the quick and the dead, to have remission of pain or guilt, were blasphemous fables, and dangerous deceits."

Just how truly Cranmer believed in these so-called "protestant doctrines", may be judged from his courage on the day of his martyrdom, March 21, 1556. Although he had earlier signed a document of penitence, under duress, he bravely revoked his recantation. As the flames leapt around him he reached out his hand that had signed the recantation, so that it might be destroyed first!

Chapter 18

European Reformers' Teaching

The Fifteenth Century

Having considered the development of eucharistic doctrine among the English Reformers we now briefly consider what was happening among their European counterparts. While there were many affinities between the English and European Reformers, some of their interpretations of the Lord's Supper were quite different. This is particularly obvious when we compare the views of, say Cranmer, with those of Luther. However, it is interesting to trace the many real links between John Wycliffe and European eucharistic theology.

The Hussites

The link between Wycliffe and the European reformers was forged by Jan Hus of Bohemia (1373-1415). Hus was a remarkable man in many ways and probably became aware of Wycliffe's views toward the end of the fourteenth century through the regular interchange of university students between Oxford and Prague. We know for example that Wycliffe's *Dialogue* and *Trialogus* were brought to Bohemia in 1402 by Jerome of Prague who was a great friend of Jan Hus.

Although Hus had much in common with Wycliffe and was quite outspoken about the views they shared, he did not see himself as a disciple of Wycliffe. In point of fact, Hus never publicly rejected the doctrine of transubstantiation. He believed that

Christ's body was present sacramentally at the Lord's Supper. He also differed from Wycliffe in his view regarding the celebrant. He believed the Eucharist was valid whatever the condition of the administrant. This of course would have been anathema to Wycliffe. Both men agreed that communion should be in both kinds and that the laity should receive the cup.

Hus' strong reforming views brought him into serious conflict with ecclesiastical authorities, although he had very strong popular support. He was summoned to appear before the Council of Constance in 1414 and was promised safe conduct. However, once there, Hus was falsely accused of Wycliffite views and not given fair opportunity to make his defense. The authorities also reneged on their promise of safety and Hus was arrested and cruelly burned at the stake as a heretic in July 1415.

Far from stifling the call for reform, the death of Hus and the subsequent martyrdom of his friend Jerome of Prague, the following year, only galvanized their followers. Aside from its political motivations the Hussite movement had strong religious overtones. Interestingly enough, for our present purposes, particular stress was laid on the right of the laity to receive the cup at the Lord's Supper. In particular, one party known as the Calixtines (so named for their party emblem, the Chalice [*calyx*: 'cup']) made their party cry, *sub utraque specie*, ("in both kinds"). As a result, they are also known to history as the Utraquists.

However we view the Hussite movement, and of course it numbered many extremists in its ranks, at least it demonstrated that the iron yoke of the Roman Catholic church could be thrown off. Furthermore, the stand John Hus took for the authority of Scripture and for the reformation of the Church, would serve in part as the inspiration for Martin Luther's work a century later. Indeed, it is noteworthy that from one of the turning points in Luther's career, his disputation with Eck in 1519, he emerged declaring, "We are all Hussites without knowing it. St. Paul and Augustine are Hussites!"

The Sixteenth Century

There were two main streams of the Reformation in Europe on the sixteenth century, the German and the Swiss. The German movement was of course initiated and directed by Martin Luther; the Swiss by Ulrich Zwingli and later, by John Calvin. While both movements were spontaneous and independent of each other indeed, sometimes vehemently opposed to each other, they had certain features in common. For example, both rejected the supremacy of the Pope; both sought the reformation of the Church by cleansing it of its abuses and corruption; and both were determined to stress the final authority of Scripture.

The main cleavage between the German and Swiss branches of the Reformation, and something which is germane to our present study, was their interpretation of the Eucharist. Both unequivocally rejected the sacrifice of the Mass and for the same basic reasons. They pointed out that since Christ's body was not "made by the priest," then there was nothing to offer in sacrifice! However, each came up with a different alternative. Luther taught his doctrine of consubstantiation while Zwingli opted for commemorationism.

Since, to a greater or lesser degree, the differences between these two streams of European thought reflected the personalities and outlooks of their respective champions, it is worth taking a closer look at these men and their beliefs. Another important factor to bear in mind is that while both men bowed to the unique authority of Scripture, each did so in his own way. Luther would do nothing that was proscribed by Scripture: Zwingli would do only what was prescribed by Scripture. These differences of emphasis are of course reflected in the German and the Swiss doctrines of the Lord's Supper.

Martin Luther, 1483 – 1546

Luther's assertion, *Sola Scriptura*, was basic to everything he taught. While he respected patristic teaching and conciliar findings, Luther declared that all must be brought to the touchstone of the Word of God. For him this Word governed the Church, not vice versa. To quote words from his, *The Babylonian Captivity of the Church*," The Church was born by the word of promise through faith.... For the Word of God is incomparably superior to the Church, and in this Word the Church, being a creature, has nothing to decree."

Having said this, it is important to recognize that despite his strong defense of the supremacy of Scripture, Luther did not originally intend to sever his relationship with the Catholic Church. His hope was to reform it in the light of Scripture. This of course proved impossible, if for no other reason than the fact that Rome considered herself to be superior to Scripture, the final interpreter of Truth.

If there is one area of his doctrine which illustrates the heart of Luther's theology, it must surely be his doctrine of the Lord's Supper. On the one hand he quite typically, sought to base his understanding of the Eucharist on Scripture, particularly on its institution by Christ. However, on the other hand, he was reluctant to abandon the traditional Catholic view concerning the real presence of Christ at the Mass. Not surprisingly therefore, it is possible to cite Luther in support of either spiritual or materialistic interpretations of the Lord's Supper.

Thus, while refuting the Thomistic doctrine of transubstantiation as unscriptural and not even properly Aristotelian, Luther nevertheless asserted that, "...it is real bread and real wine, in which Christ's real flesh and real blood are present in no other way and in no less a degree than the others (i.e. the transubstantiationalists) assert them to be under their accidents" (Works XXXVI. 29).

There can be no question that Luther made giant strides in his attempts to reform the Eucharist in Germany. For example, he not only discarded the sacrificial language of the Mass, but rejected the idea of "the sacrifice of the Mass," even ridiculing it. He writes for example, "Here standeth a wretched, brainless man at an altar and like a fool asketh that he may make an acceptable, a holy, and untouched sacrifice when he hath nothing but a morsel of bread and a sip of wine." Further, in his

Captivity, he suggests that the doctrine of the Mass is "by far the most wicked of all".

Luther saw the "confecting and offering of the body and blood of Christ" by a priest as both a blatant denial of the once-for-all, atoning work of Christ, and as an attempt to substitute human works of merit for the unmerited gift of God, namely salvation through the Cross. To use his own words: "With unheard of perversity we mock the mercy of the giver by giving as a work the thing we receive as a gift, so that the testator, instead of being a dispenser of his own goods, becomes a recipient of ours. Woe to such sacrilege!" (Works xxxvi. 48).

Obviously such statements did nothing to endear him to the religious establishment of his day.

In his biography of Luther, D'Aubigne writes about the reformer's early understanding of the Lord's Supper and records what he calls Luther's "first words uttered on a subject that has since rent the Church of the Reformation into two parties". They read as follows: "In the holy sacrament of the altar there are three things we must observe: the sign, which should be outward, visible, and in a bodily shape; the thing signified, which is inward, spiritual and in the mind of man; and faith, which makes use of both. It would be a good thing if the Church by a general council, should order both kinds to be given to the believer; not however that one kind is not sufficient, for faith alone would suffice."[28]

In the light of this statement it is surprising to discover Luther's insistence on the literal understanding of Christ's words of institution *"this is My body"*. Although he rejected the doctrine of transubstantiation, Luther believed that the body of Christ was still present at the Lord's Supper. His view, which is usually called, consubstantiation, says that while the bread and wine remain what they are, both in their accidents and substance, in some miraculous way the real, physical and whole presence of Christ is known "in, with and under" these elements. According to this view, although the glorified body of Christ is still regarded as being present in Heaven, it is said

---

28   J.H.Merle D'aubigne, *The Life and Times of Martin Luther* Chicago: Moody Press, 1978, p.287.

to be endowed with some special property of omnipresence so that it can be known alongside the bread and wine.

Despite what appears to be this rather convoluted view of the Lord's Supper, we should note that Luther insisted on the association of the Word of God and of faith with the bread and wine, in order for them to be effective. He also rejected the idea that the condition of the celebrant was inconsequential. In all fairness, we should point out that in Luther's view, the "presence of Christ" in the Eucharist was certainly not a magical consequence of a priest's words of consecration. He insisted that Christ's presence was guaranteed for all time by his own words of institution, spoken in the Upper Room *"this is My body"*.

However, it still seems that Luther must be charged with a modified *ex opere operato* view of the Eucharist. This is clear when we recognize that according to Luther's doctrine of consubstantiation, the receiving of Christ at the Lord's Supper is not only by faith, but *manducatio oralis* ("by the eating of the mouth"). It is noteworthy that although the word 'consubstantiation' is used to characterize Luther's view of the Eucharist it is not actually found in his writings.

Practically speaking, theological niceties aside, there seems to be little to choose between transubstantiation and consubstantiation. Neither view appears logical or tenable in the light of biblical Christology. After all, as noted in an earlier chapter, the deity of Christ precludes His being confined to this or that physical, geographical location, for example, "in, with or under" a loaf. By the same token Christ's glorified humanity which is present in Heaven, must not be construed as having the attribute of omnipresence, nor even ubiquity. Christian theology understands that Jesus Christ is truly God and truly man, not that He is half God and half man, nor that there is any confusing of His divine and human natures in His one Glorious Person.

Ulrich Zwingli, 1484 – 1531

Born just less than two months after Luther, on January 1,

1484, Zwingli, like his German counterpart, was widely read. However, while Luther was essentially a theologian, uncompromising in his attitude to opponents, Zwingli was a more moderate, conciliatory, humanist type of churchman. He was ordained to the priesthood in 1506 and became pastor and preacher at the influential Great Minister of Zurich in 1518.

The differences between the styles and attitudes of Luther and Zwingli are well expressed by H.M. Fairburn in his article in the Cambridge Modern History. He writes, "Luther never escaped from the feelings of the monk and associations of the cloister, but Zwingli studied his New Testament with a fine sense of the sanity of its thought, the combined practicability of its ideals and the majesty of its spirit; and his ambition was to realize a religion after its model, free from the traditions and superstitions of men. It was this that made him so tolerant of Luther, and Luther so intolerant of him. The differences of character were insuperable."[29]

Zwingli exercised considerable influence politically as well as ecclesiastically from his base in Zurich. Although he eventually resigned from his Church, he remained the controlling voice among Swiss reformers. For the purposes of our study, it is interesting to note that the same year, 1525, which saw the publishing of Zwingli's two important works: *Subsidium sive Coronis de Eucharistia* and *de Vera et Falsa Religione*, also witnessed the abolition of the Mass at Zurich.

The so-called Zwinglian view of the Lord's Supper is usually stated to be both a rejection of the Catholic and the Lutheran views, and a denial of the real presence of Christ at the Lord's Supper. It is generally agreed that Zwingli taught that the Eucharist had no sacramental efficacy but was merely a *nuda signa* (bare sign) of the relationship between the believer and his Lord.

However, in his "Reckoning and Declaration of Faith", a confessional statement delivered before the Diet of Augsburg in 1530, Zwingli makes the following statement, "I believe that in the holy supper of thanksgiving the very body of Christ is present... to the eyes and contemplation of our faith." He goes

---

29   H. M. Fairburn, *The Cambridge Modern History*, Vol. II, pp. 345,346.

on to say that, "the celebration of the sacrament is a confession of the Christian's faith that he is saved through the bodily incarnation and saving death of the Lord Jesus." From this it would appear that while Zwingli rejected the *menducatio oralis* ("eating by mouth") of both transubstantiation and consubstantiation, he did not deny the spiritual presence of Christ at the Lord's Supper. The important event at the Supper, for Zwingli, is not the priest's words of consecration; nor some magical "confecting" of Christ; nor even the eating of the bread and drinking of the wine, whether regarded as substantial or substantial without accidents, but the enjoyment of Christ by faith, as enabled by the Holy Spirit.

It is significant that Zwingli's rejection of the Catholic and Lutheran views was based on his more perceptive understanding of Christology. He pointed out that to maintain the idea of the omnipresence of Christ's physical body is to rob the Incarnation of meaning, "for nothing may be everywhere but the Godhead." This crucial observation of his has been all too lightly grasped by his critics.

Among Zwingli's other important emphases were the following: his insistence that, nothing not commanded by Scripture was binding; that the condition of the celebrant must surely effect the spiritual validity of the Eucharist; that the relation of the soul to God is more important than any liturgy and that the Lord's Supper is essentially an occasion of corporate remembrance. It is a social rather than a personal event. Zwingli believed that in the Lord's Supper we celebrate our mystical union with Christ, and demonstrate our spiritual union with other believers: here is the sacrament of unity.

Zwingli's teaching was of course anathema to Luther who not only condemned the Swiss Reformer but characterized his teaching as "of the Devil". Despite this, Zwingli was still willing to be conciliatory and agreed to discuss the issue at Marburg in 1529. The debate centered around the question: "What change is wrought by consecration in the elements?" Unfortunately, Luther was intractable and refused even to shake hands with Zwingli. A further attempt at reconciliation was made at the Diet of Basel where Bucer, another Swiss Reformer, presented the Creed of Strassbourg. This creed is also known as the "Tetrapolitana," from the four cities of Strassbourg, Constance, Memmigen and Linden which sponsored it. The key statement was that, "the true body and blood of Christ were given, truly to eat and drink, for the nourishment of souls". This time it was the Zwinglian party from Zurich, that rejected such a statement.

Whatever history's verdict on Ulrich Zwingli's views, and it is not always as kind as it might be, he was a truly Christian Reformer. In many ways he was more "reformed" than Luther and almost certainly developed his views independently. Although criticized as too subjective in his view of the Lord's Supper, Zwingli certainly encouraged its regular and general observance by all true believers. His rejection of the more mystical, quasi-magical view of the elements was a welcome redress of the balance of eucharistic doctrine and an important attempt to get back to the unadorned simplicity of the words of Christ and His apostles.

John Calvin, 1509 – 1564

The third of the European reformers to make a profound and lasting impact on eucharistic theology was John Calvin. Born in France, Calvin studied in both Paris and Orleans. He became one of the leaders of the Protestants in Paris but was obliged through persecution, to leave that city. Eventually he settled in Strassbourg, where he was able to continue his literary work, including the publication of the first edition of his, Institutes of the Christian Religion in 1536. This work, which began as a seven chapter summary of Christian doctrine, eventually became Calvin's magnum opus and grew to seventy nine chapters and was republished in 1559.

By this time of course, Calvin had established himself in Geneva, Switzerland, another great centre of the Reformation in Europe. His view of the Lord's Supper is set out in his Institutes, in various tracts and treatises as well as in his Bible commentaries and in correspondence with such contemporary reformers as Henry Bullinger and Guillaume Farel.

Calvin's view is at once, a reaction against the eucharistic doctrines of Catholicism, Lutheranism and Zwingli. He attempted to explain the significance of the Lord's Supper in the light of biblical Christology. He recognized the importance of the Breaking of Bread and was anxious to rescue it from the realm of superstition and empty ritual and to re-establish it as a regular and significant part of the life and ministry of the Church.

Calvin at first decreed, in his Articles on Church Organization and Worship at Geneva of 1537, that the Lord's Supper should be administered every Sunday. It is unfortunate that later, with a view to accommodating his followers, he adjusted this, first to a monthly and then to a quarterly observance—Christmas, Easter, Pentecost and the first Sunday in September.

Calvin rejected the Catholic view of the Mass not only as a blasphemous misrepresentation of Christ's ordinance but as both logically and theologically untenable. In his view it was absurd to think either of making or eating, the physical body of Christ. Equally repugnant to him was the idea of repeatedly offering the body and blood of Christ as a sacrifice.

Calvin's theological objection, to both the Roman Catholic doctrine of Transubstantiation and the Lutheran doctrine of consubstantiation stemmed from his understanding of biblical Christology. As an orthodox Christian he believed in Christ's essential deity and real humanity. He rightly understood that a proper view of the Lord's Supper must be controlled by an orthodox Christology.

He recognized the doctrine of the literal and whole presence of Christ in the bread of the Eucharist to be inimical to the doctrine of Christ's deity. If Christ is divine, then He cannot be bound or limited to "the corruptible elements of this world", to use Calvin's own words. Similarly, he rejected the Lutheran view as an attack on the real humanity of Christ. He understood that consubstantiation, with its corollary of the ubiquity of the physical body of Christ "in, with and under" the bread, was as much a denial of Christ's humanity as the Catholic idea of the omnipresence of Christ's body had been. Calvin had no doubt that the real, ascended body of Christ in Heaven retained all its human characteristics but he refused to confuse that body with Christ's deity or with his spiritual presence in the Eucharist. He pointed out that nothing should be detracted from Christ's "... heavenly glory, as happens when He is brought under the corruptible elements of this world or bound to any earthly creatures. Nothing inappropriate to human nature (should) be ascribed to His body, as happens when it is said to be infinite or to be put in a number of places at once." (Institutes iv. 12.19.)

Calvin made his most significant contribution to the doctrine of the Lord's Supper in his teaching about the "spiritual presence of Christ." While recognizing that the elements used in communion are symbols, Calvin insisted that what was symbolized, namely the body and blood of Christ, was also present spiritually. The symbol was the outward, visible evidence of the unseen reality. In this sense the Supper becomes a sacrament or pledge of the real though unseen, presence of the Saviour. By insisting on the actual, spiritual presence of Christ at the Eucharist, Calvin clearly repudiated Zwingli's memorialism.

He avoided the materialism of the doctrines of transubstantiation and consubstantiation by distinguishing between the physical, local presence of Christ in Heaven and His spiritual presence in the Eucharist, mysteriously made real to the believer by the Holy Spirit. He understood Christ's words of institution *"this is My body... this is My blood"* literally but sacramentally. While there was no change of the physical substance of the bread and wine, either in themselves nor by any additions to them, they are Christ's body and blood to the believing communicant. They are spiritual food by which we are nourished. Of course, it goes without saying that Calvin saw the necessity of communion in both kinds. He recognized that withholding of the cup from the laity was the withholding of half of their spiritual food. Here are some of Calvin's own words: "...We neither make the sign the thing, nor confound both in one, nor enclose the Body of Christ in the bread, nor, on the other hand, imagine it to be infinite, nor dream of a carnal transfusion of Christ into us, nor lay down any other fiction of that sort." [30]

To understanding the difference between Calvin's and Zwingli's teaching, we need to keep in mind that while both recognized the bread and wine to be symbols, Zwingli saw them as that alone, while Calvin saw them as a sacrament through which Christ was communicated to the believer by the Holy Spirit. Typically, Calvin distrusted faith as too subjective and as suggesting some virtue in man. He preferred to rest his case on divine grace and the work of the Spirit of God.

By insisting on the spiritual presence of Christ in the Lord's Supper, Calvin does two things. First, he remains true to his belief in the full deity and the full humanity of Christ. He avoids two errors, localizing the Saviour's deity and ubiquitizing His humanity. Christ is still in heaven yet, the benefits of His passion and humanity are available to His people on earth. Second, he retains the significance and importance of the communion service, and prevents its becoming as he says "frivolous and useless". He argues that, "...the sacraments of the Lord should not and cannot be at all separated from their reality and substance. To distinguish, in order to guard against confounding them, is not only good and reasonable, but altogether necessary; but to divide them, so as to make the one exist without the other, is absurd." [31]

Although Calvin understood the application of the sacrament to be singularly the ministry of the Holy Spirit, he still recognizes the need for faith. For example, he saw no benefit in the Lord's Supper, for an unbeliever. Indeed he warned against encouraging unbelievers to participate in communion lest they eat and drink to their own condemnation. In Calvin's view a minister who "knowingly and willingly admits an unworthy person whom he could rightfully turn away, is as guilty of sacrilege as if he cast the Lord's body to dogs." [32]

The believing faith of a Christian is essential for two reasons,

30   Ed Jules Bonnet, *Letters of Calvin*, (New York: Burt Franklin Reprints, n.d. p.170.
31   Calvin, *Institutes of Religion* iv xvii. 10 p.1371.
32   Ibid. xii. 11

at least. First, in Calvin's view, the blessings of the sacrament are only enjoyed by the person who has trusted in Christ and His death for salvation. And, second, only the man of faith can receive the truth of the mystery that, while Christ is literally present in Heaven, He is spiritually present in His Feast, here on earth. In other words the Lord's Supper is a Means of Grace, communicated by the Spirit, received by faith. Calvin believed in a two way communion. On the one hand, the communicant directs his thoughts to the Risen Lord; on the other, the Spirit applies the spiritual effect of the body and blood of Christ to the believing communicant. The Supper thus becomes a time of receiving and a time of responding. Calvin's view of the Lord's Supper is sometimes characterized as "virtualism", from his suggestion that the Supper is a Means of Grace through which the believer receives the power or virtue of the body and blood of Christ.

This is not to be construed in some physical or quasi-physical sense but only in a spiritual one. While Calvin's teaching comes somewhere between that of Luther and Zwingli, he appears to be closer in thought to Luther. We can summarize Calvin's teaching in his own words: "...it is not necessary that the essence of the flesh should descend from Heaven in order to our being fed upon it, the virtue of the Spirit being sufficient to break through all impediments and surmount any distance of place. Meanwhile we deny not that this mode is incomprehensible to the human mind; because neither can flesh naturally be the life of the soul, nor exert its power upon us from Heaven, nor without reason is the communion which makes us flesh of the flesh of Christ, and bone of His bones, called by Paul, 'A great mystery' (Eph. 5:30). Therefore, in the sacred Supper we acknowledge a miracle which surpasses both the limits of nature and the measure of our sense, while the life of Christ is common to us, and His flesh is given us for food. But we must have done with all inventions inconsistent with the explanation lately given, such as the ubiquity of the body, the secret inclosing under the symbol of bread, and the substantial presence on earth ." (*Tracts*, II, 577).

In the foregoing, brief historical review we have looked at the development of the different eucharistic traditions from the days of the Early Church, down to the Reformation. Obviously, we have given more space to the English and European Reformers' teaching than to that of the followers of Thomas Aquinas. Particular attention has been given to the thoughts of men like John Wycliffe, Martin Luther, Ulrich Zwingli and John Calvin.

Although there have been a variety of emphases and practical applications of the doctrine of the Lord's Supper since the Reformation, there has been very little theological development in this subject. The four main positions remain. First, there is the persisting Roman Catholic view that, upon the priest's consecration, the actual body and blood of Christ take the place of the material emblems. Second, there is the Lutheran view that the physical body and blood of Christ are present "in, with and under" the bread and wine. Third, there is the "Reformed" (Calvinist) view that while the bread and wine remain just that, they are sacramental: a means of grace through which Christ is communicated by the Holy Spirit, to quicken and strengthen faith. Fourth, there is the "Zwinglian" view, which while stressing the importance of the regular celebration of the Lord's Supper, by true believers, regards the elements simply as commemorative symbols. On this view, the bread and wine, while reminding the believer of Christ's death, burial, resurrection, coming, and abiding presence, are not in themselves means of grace, except in a secondary sense.

While no reference has been made to it, if only for the reason that it adds nothing to our understanding of the Lord's Supper, there is another view. It is sometimes rather inappropriately called the "mystical view". A relic of Quietism, it suggests that the Lord's Supper was not intended as an ongoing part of Church life, but was given merely as an aid to faith in the Primitive, primarily Jewish church. Truly mature Christian experience, this view alleges, no longer needs visual, material aids. Viewed in the light of Scripture and in particular, Christ's own words of institution, this view can hardly be considered to be a Christian view of the Lord's Supper.

It is unfortunate that the Reformers in their rebuttal of the blasphemous and idolatrous doctrines of the Roman Mass, failed to achieve theological consensus. However, it is important to recognize two things. First, because of the atmosphere of the times; the superstition of the common people and the overwhelming power and authority of the Catholic Church, the Reformers were necessarily cast in the role of polemicists. Their every move was condemned: their every word disapproved. This meant that in their desire to give accurate expression to their theology and their understanding of Scripture, they sometimes overstated their case and appeared to be in opposition to one another. Second, despite their strident tones and intolerance of contrary opinions, the Reformers had far more points of agreement in the essentials of eucharistic doctrine, than is sometimes allowed. For example, without exception, they all rejected the superstition that a mere man, call him a "priest" or whatever, was able to "confect" or "make" the actual, physical body of Christ. Furthermore, they all rejected out of hand, the notion that there could be any repeating of the sacrifice of Christ in order to achieve the forgiveness of sins. They all believed that the cup as well as the bread, be given to every communicant.

Thus, the Reformers had far more points in common than in contention. Their concern was to be loyal to the Word of God and faithful to the Saviour's words of institution. They all recognized the work of the Holy Spirit and the importance of true saving faith in Christ's "once-for-all," redeeming sacrifice.

It is comparatively easy for us to be critical of our spiritual forbears from the comfortable pew of twenty first century Christianity. It must have been much more difficult to think biblically and act definitively, when struggling against persecution and the tide of entrenched, politically motivated, medieval ecclesiasticism. Let us be grateful that devoted, thoughtful followers of Christ were willing, even at the risk of life and limb, to preserve for us, a clear and scriptural understanding of the truth regarding the Lord's Supper. They were at least as concerned as we, to *"keep the Feast, not with the old yeast, the yeast of malice and wickedness, but with bread without yeast, the bread of sincerity and truth"* (1 Cor.5:8).

9 781926 765259